The Official Netflix Cookbook

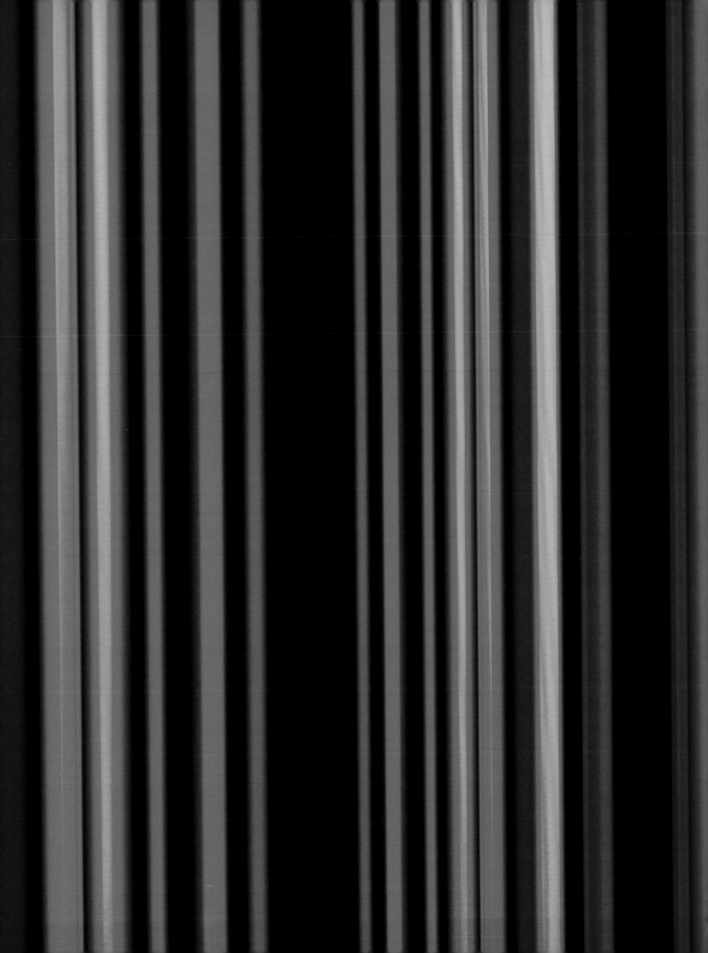

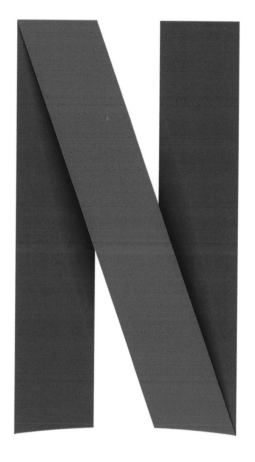

The Official Netflix Cookbook

70 Recipes from Your TV to Your Table

ANNA PAINTER

PHOTOGRAPHY BY **BERYL STRIEWSKI**

INSIGHT
EDITIONS

SAN RAFAEL · LOS ANGELES · LONDON

Contents

1

TUDUM: Appetizers and Small Plates

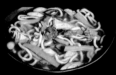
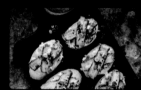

8 WATCH PARTY: Bridgerton

9 Sweet Inspirations

Foreword

I love cookbooks. I read them straight through like a novel, luxuriating in the development of the themes and rising to the challenges laid out in their glossy pages. In my mind's eye, I then serve everything from my gleaming clean kitchen to my applauding friends and adoring family. (Well, a girl can dream, can't she?)

Cooking and baking for loved ones is the ultimate act of caretaking, the pinnacle of cozy, the most together-ing thing you can offer, right? I know enjoying a home-cooked meal really centers my family. Our favorite weekend nights take us straight from the kitchen table to the couch to snuggle up and watch the latest and greatest (or even old favorites) on Netflix.

I was lucky enough to develop and make *Yes Day* with Netflix, a process I loved. Producing a movie for families felt like making a meal for my own, as we carefully gathered just the right ingredients: Take one beloved book by Amy Krouse Rosenthal (not to mention one of my kids' favorite traditions), stir in the glamour (Jenna Ortega and Edgar Ramirez, ooh la la), combine with a rip-roaring script (Kablowey anyone?), and you are officially cooking up something fun. We were beyond thrilled to see *Yes Day* bring comfort and togetherness to families all around the world, especially during the dimmed fun of pandemic living.

To me, *The Official Netflix Cookbook* makes perfect sense. We are all hoping to end our day enjoying Netflix anyway, so cooking on theme just takes the experience up a notch! Like Netflix, this cookbook is global, with recipes like Gabriel's Coq au Vin from *Emily in Paris* and Haengbok Noodles from *Extraordinary Attorney Woo*. Plus, a couple funny ones, for example Tea Fit for a Lady from *Bridgerton* and "Is It a Hamburger or Is It Cake?" It also includes watch parties for favorites like *Stranger Things* and *Squid Game*. With 70 recipes, it is so many things, but mostly it is about connecting with people you love.

While I love to read straight through cookbooks, it never occurred to me to watch my way through a cookbook before. But that's exactly what I am going to do, thanks to *The Official Netflix Cookbook*. My kids and I will report back when we've made (and watched!) everything. Maybe we will celebrate with the *Yes Day*'s Gut-Buster Parfait!

Have fun and bon appétit!

Love,

Jen Garner xxx

Introduction

For more than 25 years, Netflix has helped audiences find their next favorite story amongst thousands of genres, everything from action & adventure and horror to romantic comedies and reality competitions. Streaming in more than 37 languages and 190 countries, Netflix knows that great stories can come from anywhere and be loved everywhere. Whatever you like and no matter where you live, Netflix has a series, documentary, feature film, or mobile game perfect for you. Plus, the service's seemingly ideal recommendations enable you to discover your next obsession, as well as watch what you love, whenever you want. So, what could possibly make this immersive experience better? Why food, of course!

Netflix has teamed up with Anna Painter to bring you delicious recipes inspired by some of your favorite shows and movies. *The Official Netflix Cookbook* serves up appetizers, meals, desserts, and drinks for the ultimate snacking and streaming experience. Want to gossip at a *Bridgerton*-themed high tea? Dying to challenge your friends to ask, "*Is It Cake?*" Want to host a home version of *Iron Chef*? Need an idea for a romantic dinner for an *Emily in Paris* binge? Want a mind-flaying drink that evokes the horror of the Upside Down from *Stranger Things*? Featuring 70 recipes to fit every watching mood, there's all of that and more within these pages.

Like Netflix's streaming service, this cookbook features food from around the world and dishes everyone can enjoy. Each recipe ties into a special moment or theme for their stories, such as movies like *Roma* and *The Sea Beast* to reality competitions such as *Great British Baking Show* and *Nailed It!* to thrilling series including *Squid Game* and *Ozark*. Are some recipes more difficult than others? Sure! But where possible we've added tips and swaps for when you are short on time. Perfect for watch parties, weekend marathons, or when you are just feeling snacky, the recipes in our cookbook are sure to enhance your viewing experience and possibly introduce you to your next favorite show. So let's dive in!

The Netflix Timeline

1997 ●───────────────────────────────────────

1997: Reed Hastings and Marc Randolph come up with the idea of renting DVDs by mail

1998: Netflix.com launches, first DVD shipped is *Beetlejuice*

1999: Netflix subscription service debuts

2000: Personalized movie recommendation system is introduced

2003: Subscription rental membership surpasses 1 million

2005: Profiles feature for different users launched

2007: Netflix begins streaming

2010: Streaming launches on mobile devices

2012: Netflix reaches 25 million members

2013: First slate of original programming debuts, including *House of Cards*, which wins an Emmy, the first for an Internet streaming service

2014: Surpasses 50 million members

2016: Netflix expands to 130 countries, bringing the service to members in 190 countries and 21 languages

2017: Hits 100 million members globally; wins first Academy Award for *The White Helmets*

2020: Top 10 list debuts; Netflix is the most-nominated studio in the Academy Awards and Emmys

2021: Surpasses 200 million members

2022: 25th anniversary of launch; hosts Netflix Is a Joke: The Festival

2023: Netflix streams its first-ever live show, *Chris Rock: Selective Outrage*

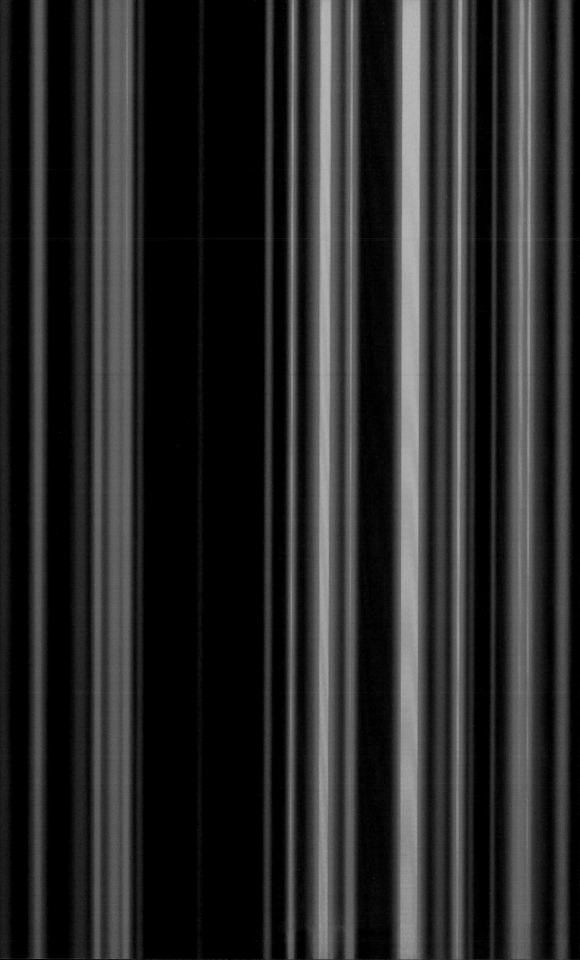

TUDUM:
Appetizers and Small Plates

Just as every good story on Netflix begins with the iconic "Tudum" sound, every good meal starts with an amazing appetizer, small plate, or cocktail.

Crispy "Glass Onion" Rings with Hot Honey Dipping Sauce

In *Glass Onion: A Knives Out Mystery*, a puzzle-box invitation leads Detective Benoit Blanc to join a wealthy tech executive's group of friends on his private island in Greece. There, a murder mystery game turns deadly, leading Blanc to do some quick thinking with hot sauce.

While making onion rings might not be on par with solving a murder, it is a delicate but thrilling task. Sure, you may not have a criminal in handcuffs in the end, but you will have something more delicious: beautifully golden brown, crisp onion rings drizzled in a spicy-sweet hot honey that shines like glass.

YIELD: 4 servings   **PREP TIME:** 10 minutes   **COOK TIME:** 40 minutes    **VEGETARIAN**

1 large sweet onion (Vidalia or Walla Walla)

1 cup cornstarch, divided

1 cup all-purpose flour

1 teaspoon baking powder

¼ teaspoon baking soda

1 teaspoon smoked paprika

Kosher salt and freshly ground black pepper

Vegetable oil for frying

¾ cup cold beer, preferably lager or pilsner*

¼ cup cold seltzer

½ cup honey

1 teaspoon hot sauce, more or less depending on heat preferences

1 lemon, cut into wedges

*For a nonalcoholic option, use ¾ cup cold seltzer in place of the beer.

1   Preheat the oven to 200°F/93°C. Set a wire rack over a rimmed baking sheet.

2   Peel the onion, then cut a very thin slice off one side of the onion to create a flat surface. Balance the onion on this flat surface, then cut it crosswise into ½-inch slices. Carefully separate the slices into rings.

3   Add ½ cup of the cornstarch and a pinch of salt to a large resealable plastic bag. In a large bowl, combine the remaining ½ cup of cornstarch, flour, baking powder, baking soda, and smoked paprika. Season with the salt and pepper, then whisk until combined.

4   In a large Dutch oven, bring 2 inches of vegetable oil to 375°F/190°C over medium-high heat.

5   Meanwhile, whisk the beer and seltzer into the flour mixture. The batter should have the texture of thin pancake batter. (If the batter is too thick, add more seltzer, 1 tablespoon at a time.)

6   Once the oil is at 375°F/190°C, place a few onion rings in the bag with the cornstarch. Seal the bag, then gently shake to coat the rings in the cornstarch. Shake the excess cornstarch off the onion rings, then add them to the beer batter. Lift the rings one at a time out of the batter, letting the excess drip back into the bowl. Carefully transfer them to the hot oil, being careful not to crowd the pan.

7   Fry the onion rings, turning occasionally, for 2 to 3 minutes, until puffed and golden brown. Place on the wire rack and season generously with salt; transfer the baking sheet to the oven to keep the onion rings warm. Repeat with the remaining onion rings and batter.

8   In a small microwave-safe bowl, combine the honey and hot sauce. Heat on high, in 15-second increments, until the honey is warm and loose. Squeeze the lemon wedges over the onion rings and drizzle with the hot honey mixture.

SOMEBODY FEED PHIL

NYC Pizza Bites

On *Somebody Feed Phil*, the ever-smiling and ever-curious Phil Rosenthal is always on the hunt for something delicious. The New York episode brings Phil to the famed Brooklyn restaurant Di Fara Pizza, where owner Dom DeMarco makes him one of his famous pies, snipping fresh basil over the pie just before serving it.

Here we make a mini bite-sized version of this iconic New York pizza. Go all in and make your own dough and sauce or use store-bought (see page 17), but don't skip the freshly snipped basil on top!

YIELD: 16 pizza bites
PREP TIME: 15 minutes, plus rising time
COOK TIME: 1 hour

 VEGETARIAN

"Food is the great connector and laughs are the cement."

—PHIL ROSENTHAL

PIZZA DOUGH

¾ cup warm water

1 envelope (¼ ounce) active dry yeast

2 teaspoons honey

2 tablespoons olive oil, plus more for brushing and drizzling

1 teaspoon kosher salt

2 cups all-purpose flour

PIZZA SAUCE

2 teaspoons olive oil

1 tablespoon butter

1 garlic clove, finely chopped

One 15-ounce can whole peeled tomatoes

½ teaspoon dried oregano

½ teaspoon granulated sugar

1 small bunch fresh basil (about ½ ounce), divided

Kosher salt and freshly ground black pepper

8 ounces whole-milk mozzarella, coarsely grated

1 ounce Parmesan cheese, grated

Olive oil for drizzling

Crushed red pepper flakes (optional)

1 **To make the pizza dough:** Pour ¾ cup of warm water in a medium bowl. Sprinkle the yeast over the top and let it stand for about 5 minutes, until the yeast is foamy. Whisk in the honey, 2 tablespoons of olive oil, and salt. Add the flour, ½ cup at a time, stirring with a rubber spatula until a sticky dough forms.

2 Place the dough in a large, lightly oiled bowl, turning the dough to coat it in oil. Cover the bowl with a clean tea towel and let the dough rest at room temperature for 1 to 2 hours, until doubled in size.

3 **To make the pizza sauce:** In a medium saucepan, heat the olive oil and butter over medium. When the butter has melted, add the garlic and cook for about 1 minute, until fragrant. Pour the tomatoes and their juices into the pan, breaking the tomatoes into bite-sized pieces with a wooden spoon. Add the oregano, sugar, and one sprig of basil to the saucepan. Season with ¼ teaspoon of kosher salt and a few grinds of fresh pepper. Reduce the heat to low and cook, stirring occasionally, for about 30 minutes, until the sauce is thick and flavorful. Remove from the heat and season to taste with additional salt and pepper.

4 **To make the pizza bites:** On a lightly floured surface, knead the pizza dough a few times, then shape it into a smooth ball. Divide the ball into four pieces, then divide each quarter into four pieces. Shape each piece into a small ball. Transfer the dough balls to a lightly floured work surface, cover with the same clean tea towel, and let rest for 15 minutes.

5 Preheat the oven to 450°F/232°C. Place the racks in the center and lower third positions. Line two rimmed baking sheets with parchment paper.

6 Working one at a time, roll or stretch each piece of dough into a 2-inch round. (Keep the other dough balls covered.) Transfer to the prepared baking sheets, then repeat with the remaining dough.

7 Top each round with the pizza sauce, mozzarella, and Parmesan. Drizzle all of the pizza bites with olive oil and season with crushed red pepper flakes, if using.

8 Transfer the pizza bites to the oven and bake for 15 to 20 minutes, or until the crusts are golden brown and the cheese is melted and bubbling. Be sure to rotate the baking sheets from top to bottom halfway through baking.

9 Remove the pizza bites from the oven. Drizzle with a little more olive oil, and then, using kitchen scissors, snip the remaining fresh basil over the top.

▶▶ **Fast forward**

Short on time for home-made pizza dough and simmered tomato sauce? Use a 1-pound ball of store-bought pizza dough and 1 cup of your favorite marinara sauce. Cold pizza dough is more difficult to shape, so let the dough rest at room temperature for at least 30 minutes, preferably 1 to 2 hours, before beginning to shape.

THE
SEA BEAST

Coconut Shrimp with Two Dipping Sauces

After an epic battle with the infamous sea beast, monster hunter Jacob and the castaway Maisie are on a boat that is nearly swallowed by the creature known as the Red Bluster. Instead of being eaten, they are brought to a desert island and Jacob has to find food for the two. First, the pair eat coconuts. Then, Red helps them hunt small fish using a technique known as bubble-net feeding.

Inspired by Jacob's attempts at dinner, we created an easy, crispy coconut shrimp, sure to please both pint-sized stowaways and larger-than-life monster hunters alike. As a nod to Red, who was more friend than foe in the end, we created two quick dipping sauces, a bright-hued sweet chili sauce and spicy mayo. Both sauces can be made ahead of time and refrigerated in sealed containers for up to two days, but the shrimp should be fried just before serving.

YIELD: 4 servings
PREP TIME: 30 minutes
COOK TIME: 15 minutes

SWEET CHILI DIPPING SAUCE

½ cup sweet Thai chili sauce

3 tablespoons apricot preserves or orange marmalade

1 lime

SPICY MAYO

1 garlic clove, peeled and finely grated

⅔ cup mayonnaise

2 to 3 teaspoons chili garlic sauce

Kosher salt and freshly ground black pepper

COCONUT SHRIMP

1 pound large, peeled and deveined shrimp

Kosher salt and freshly ground black pepper

⅔ cup all-purpose flour

2 large eggs

2 cups unsweetened shredded coconut

1 cup panko bread crumbs

Vegetable oil for frying

1 **To make the sweet chili dipping sauce:** In a small bowl, combine the sweet Thai chili sauce and the apricot preserves or marmalade. Halve the lime, squeeze one half into the dipping sauce, then stir to combine. Cut the other half into wedges and reserve for serving.

2 **To make the spicy mayo:** To a small bowl, add garlic, mayo, and chili garlic sauce. Stir to combine, then season to taste with salt and pepper.

3 **To make the coconut shrimp:** Pat the shrimp dry, then season with a pinch each of salt and pepper. Add the flour to a large resealable plastic bag, then season with salt and pepper. In a medium shallow bowl, crack the eggs, then whisk to combine. Line a large plate with paper towels to drain the cooked shrimp.

4 Place the shrimp in the bag, then seal and shake it until the shrimp are completely coated with flour. Transfer the shrimp to a plate, shaking off the excess flour back into the bag as you work. Discard the flour from the bag, then add the coconut, bread crumbs, and a pinch each of salt and pepper to the same bag. Shake the bag to combine the ingredients.

>>recipe continues on next page

NETFLIX

WATCH
THE SEA BEAST

>>Coconut Shrimp with Two Dipping Sauces continued

5 Add half of the shrimp to the bowl with the beaten eggs, then using a fork or slotted spoon, lift the shrimp out of the egg, allowing the excess egg to drip back into the bowl. Transfer these shrimp to the bag with the coconut and bread crumbs, then seal and shake to coat the shrimp. (The shrimp will not be fully covered by the coconut mixture.) Place the shrimp on a second plate, then pat gently to help the coating adhere. Repeat with the remaining shrimp.

6 In a large nonstick skillet, heat ¼ inch of vegetable oil over medium-high. When the oil is shimmering, add half of the shrimp to the skillet. Cook, 2 to 3 minutes per side, turning once, until the coconut mixture is golden brown and the shrimp are cooked through. Transfer to the paper towel–lined plate and season to taste with salt. Repeat with the remaining shrimp, adding more oil to the skillet if necessary.

7 Squeeze the lime wedges over the cooked shrimp, then serve with the dipping sauces.

Cobra Kai
Mini Sloppy Johnnys

When making dinner, Johnny Lawrence of *Cobra Kai* tastes the sloppy joe mixture he's cooking in a skillet, mutters "not manly enough," and adds the rest of a bag of beef jerky. Adding the jerky may be an unconventional addition to the classic sandwich but maybe Johnny is onto something here?

For our version, which is perfect fuel for a *Cobra Kai* marathon, we make sliders and top the sloppy joe with a beef jerky filling that includes chopped onion, pickles, and potato chips for extra karate crunch.

YIELD: 12 sliders   **PREP TIME:** 10 minutes   **COOK TIME:** 30 minutes

1 small onion

1 tablespoon unsalted butter, plus more for brushing

1 pound ground beef

Kosher salt and freshly ground black pepper

1 green pepper, seeded and finely chopped

2 garlic cloves, finely chopped

1 ounce beef jerky, finely chopped (optional)

1 cup ketchup

1 tablespoon dark brown sugar

1 tablespoon Worcestershire sauce

1 tablespoon spicy brown or Dijon mustard

1 to 2 teaspoons dark chili powder, depending on your heat preference

A few dashes hot sauce (optional)

12 slider buns, halved

Sliced dill pickles or spicy pickled peppers for serving

Potato chips for serving

1   Peel and finely chop the onion. Reserve ¼ cup of onion for step 5. In a large skillet over medium-high heat, melt 1 tablespoon of the butter, then add the ground beef. Season with 1 teaspoon of salt and a few grinds of pepper. Cook, stirring occasionally, for about 8 minutes, until the beef is browned and cooked through. Carefully spoon off the accumulated fat.

2   Add the onion, pepper, and garlic to the beef. Cook, stirring occasionally, for about 3 minutes, until the vegetables have softened.

3   Add the beef jerky, if desired, ketchup, ½ cup water, brown sugar, Worcestershire sauce, mustard, and chili powder. Bring to a simmer, then reduce the heat to low. Cook, stirring occasionally, for about 15 minutes, until the sauce has reduced slightly and is thick and flavorful. Season the sloppy johnny mixture with salt and pepper to taste and, if desired, the hot sauce.

4   Preheat the broiler. Arrange the buns, cut side up, on a rimmed baking sheet. Brush the cut sides with melted butter. Broil for about 2 minutes, until the buns are warm and lightly toasted. (Watch closely as broilers vary.)

5   Divide the sloppy johnny mixture among the toasted rolls and top with the reserved raw onion, dill pickles or spicy pickled peppers, and a few potato chips. Serve the remaining chips on the side.

INVENTING
ANNA

Mushroom Risotto Bites

MUSHROOM RISOTTO

½ cup dried porcini mushrooms

1 cup boiling water

8 ounces white button mushrooms, stemmed

2 tablespoons olive oil

1 shallot, peeled and finely chopped

Kosher salt and freshly ground black pepper

2 large garlic cloves, peeled and finely chopped

1 cup arborio rice

½ cup white wine

2 cups vegetable broth

1 ounce Parmesan cheese, divided

RISOTTO BITES

1 small bunch fresh chives (about ¼ ounce)

1 small bunch fresh parsley (about ¼ ounce)

2 large eggs

2 ounces fontina cheese, coarsely grated

½ cup panko bread crumbs

Vegetable oil for frying

Kosher salt

1 lemon, cut into wedges

At Hotel 12 George in New York, the staff caters to their wealthy guests' whims, from procuring exclusive reservations to placing their names on every VIP list. One day, Anna Delvey enters the hotel, tipping all the staff in one-hundred-dollar bills, including Neff, the concierge. They become friends, with Anna inviting Neff into the glittering world she has created for herself by being either a con artist or an audacious entrepreneur, depending on who you believe.

To fortify yourself to watch all of *Inventing Anna*, you will need a glass of something bubbly and a platter of elegant, bite-sized snacks like those served at the cocktail bar in 12 George. May we suggest these rich, delicious risotto cakes? The risotto can be made ahead of time, and then the individual risotto cakes can be pan-fried just before you start the next episode.

YIELD: 24 risotto bites
PREP TIME: 35 minutes, plus soaking
COOK TIME: 1 hour 15 minutes

🌱 VEGETARIAN

1 **To make the mushroom risotto:** Place the dried mushrooms in a medium heatproof bowl. Pour the boiling water over them, then let sit at room temperature for about 30 minutes, until the mushrooms have softened. Drain and reserve the mushroom soaking liquid, then finely chop the mushrooms.

2 Preheat the oven to 425°F/218°C with a rack in the center position. Thinly slice the white button mushroom caps.

3 In a medium ovenproof Dutch oven, heat the olive oil over medium-high. Place the shallots in the Dutch oven and season with a pinch each of salt and pepper. Cook for 2 to 3 minutes, until softened. Add the garlic, sliced button mushrooms, and soaked porcini mushrooms to the Dutch oven. Cook for 3 to 4 minutes, stirring occasionally, until the mushrooms are tender.

4 Add the rice to the Dutch oven, then cook, stirring, for 1 to 2 minutes, until the rice is toasted. Add the wine and cook, stirring, for about 30 seconds, until the liquid is absorbed. Stir the mushroom soaking liquid, vegetable broth, and ½ teaspoon of salt into the rice and bring to a boil over high heat.

5 Remove the Dutch oven from the heat, cover, and transfer to the oven. Bake for about 20 minutes, until the liquid has absorbed and the rice is tender.

6 While the risotto bakes, finely grate the Parmesan. Reserve ¼ cup of the cheese for garnishing the risotto cakes, then stir the remaining Parmesan into the cooked risotto.

7 Season the risotto with salt and pepper to taste. Transfer to the refrigerator and cool completely, at least 2 hours, preferably overnight.

8 **To make the risotto bites:** Preheat the oven to 200°F/93°C. Finely chop the chives and the parsley leaves and stems. Reserve 1 tablespoon of each herb for garnishing.

9 Lightly beat the eggs. To a medium bowl, add 3 cups of risotto, the eggs, fontina, chopped chives and parsley, and bread crumbs. Stir to combine.

10 Roll a 2-tablespoon portion of the risotto into a ball, then gently shape into a patty. Repeat with the remaining risotto. (You should have 24 patties.)

11 Set a wire rack over a rimmed baking sheet. In a large nonstick skillet, heat 3 tablespoons vegetable oil over medium-high until shimmering. Working in batches, place the risotto cakes in the skillet. Cook for 3 to 4 minutes per side, until golden brown on both sides. Transfer to the wire rack and season with salt. Keep warm in the oven. Repeat with the remaining risotto cakes, adding additional oil as needed.

12 Transfer the risotto bites to a serving platter. Squeeze one lemon wedge over the risotto cakes, then garnish with the reserved Parmesan, chives, and parsley. Serve the remaining lemon wedges on the side.

"You're SO Basic"

SCHOOL – OF – CHOCOLATE

Coffee Truffles

On *School of Chocolate*, celebrated pastry chef Amaury Guichon coaches and encourages eight pastry students through a series of challenges designed to hone their skills and determine which one in the group is truly best in class.

While Juan Gutierrez's final showstopping piece was a magical dinosaur emerging from a prehistoric jungle, the inspiration for these coffee truffles is from Gutierrez's winning dessert on episode seven. On the episode, "Give Me Some Sugar," Gutierrez made a stunning coffee dessert that celebrated the flavors of café con leche.

For our truffles, we steep heavy cream with whole coffee beans before pouring the fragrant liquid over bittersweet chocolate. (Chef Guichon might give you bonus points if you use coffee beans from Gutierrez's native Colombia.) On *School of Chocolate*, truffles might be dipped in a tempered chocolate or a marbled mirror glaze. Here, we roll the truffles in unsweetened cocoa powder, a delicious and fuss-free finish.

YIELD: About 20 truffles
PREP TIME: 10 minutes
COOK TIME: 1 hour 40 minutes, plus 1 hour 10 minutes chilling

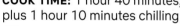 **VEGETARIAN**

¾ cup heavy cream

¼ cup dark roast whole coffee beans

1 vanilla bean, split lengthwise, or 1 cinnamon stick (optional)

12 ounces bittersweet chocolate, finely chopped

2 teaspoons coffee liqueur (optional)

⅔ cup unsweetened cocoa powder, plus more for dusting

1 In a medium saucepan, combine the heavy cream, coffee beans, and vanilla bean or cinnamon stick, if desired. Simmer over medium heat for about 5 minutes. Remove the mixture from the heat and let it steep for 30 minutes. Meanwhile, place the chocolate in a medium heatproof bowl.

2 Bring the cream mixture just to a boil over medium-high heat, about 3 minutes. Pour the warm cream through a fine-mesh sieve into the bowl with the chopped chocolate. Discard the coffee beans and the vanilla bean or cinnamon stick. Add the coffee liqueur, if desired, to the same bowl. Let stand for 10 minutes, then whisk until smooth.

3 Transfer the bowl to the refrigerator, then stir every 10 minutes for about 50 minutes, until the mixture is thick enough to scoop but still pliable.

4 Line a rimmed baking sheet with parchment paper or aluminum foil. Using a tablespoon, scoop the truffle mixture into balls, transferring them to the prepared baking sheet as you work. Place the baking sheet in the refrigerator and chill the truffles for 10 to 15 minutes, until somewhat firm but still tacky on the outside.

5 Place the cocoa powder in a shallow bowl or pie plate. Remove the portioned truffles from the refrigerator. Dust your hands with a little cocoa powder. Working a few at a time, roll the truffle balls in the cocoa powder to coat, then return to the same baking sheet.

6 Chill the cocoa-dusted truffles for 5 minutes before serving. The finished truffles can be kept in a sealed container in a cool kitchen for about 5 days. (Hot weather? Keep the truffles in a sealed container in the refrigerator.)

OUTER BANKS

The Wreck Mini Crab Cakes

In the teen drama *Outer Banks*, Kiara's parents own a restaurant called The Wreck that caters to the island's elite residents. Kiara often brings Pogue best friends here to chow down on food that's left over at the end of the night. Seafood is often on the menu in real-life Outer Banks restaurants, so these bite-sized mini crab cakes are the perfect themed snack to enjoy as you follow the adventures of JJ, John B, Rafe, Sarah, Pope, Cleo, and the rest as they search for lost gold and buried treasures.

The crab is the real star of the show in this recipe, so be sure to use the best-quality jumbo lump crabmeat you can find. A garlicky aioli is great for dipping, but you can stick with your favorite tartar sauce or ketchup if you prefer.

YIELD: 4 servings
PREP TIME: 20 minutes
COOK TIME: 30 minutes

1 small bunch fresh chives (about ¼ ounce)

1 small bunch fresh parsley (about ¼ ounce)

1 stalk celery

1 lemon

1 pound jumbo lump crabmeat

1¼ cups mayonnaise, divided

1 garlic clove

Kosher salt and freshly ground black pepper

1 teaspoon Dijon mustard

½ teaspoon Worcestershire sauce

A few dashes hot sauce

2 cups panko bread crumbs, divided

Vegetable oil for frying

NETFLIX

WATCH
OUTER BANKS

1 Finely chop the chives, parsley leaves and stems, and celery. Finely grate ½ teaspoon of lemon zest, then cut the lemon into wedges. Place the crabmeat in a medium bowl, then remove any shells or pieces of cartilage. Keep the crab cold until ready to use.

2 In a small bowl, combine ¾ cup of the mayonnaise and the juice of one lemon wedge. Finely chop the garlic clove, then add it to the mayonnaise. Season the aioli with salt and pepper to taste, then refrigerate until ready to serve.

3 In a medium bowl, combine the chopped parsley, celery, lemon zest, mustard, Worcestershire sauce, hot sauce, the remaining ½ cup of mayonnaise, and half of the chives. Stir to combine, then season with salt and pepper. Fold in the crabmeat and ¾ cup of the bread crumbs, being careful not to break up the crab too much. Place the remaining 1¼ cups of bread crumbs in a medium shallow bowl.

4 Using a ¼-cup measuring cup, scoop the crab cake mixture into small patties, then add to the bread crumbs. Coat each crab cake with some of the crumbs, pressing gently with your hands to help the crumbs adhere. Transfer the breaded crab cakes to a large plate or baking sheet. Line a second large plate with paper towels.

5 In a large nonstick skillet, heat 2 tablespoons of vegetable oil over medium-high until shimmering. Working in batches, add the crab cakes to the skillet and cook for 2 to 3 minutes per side, flipping once, until the crab cakes are golden brown on both sides. Transfer the cooked crab cakes to the paper towel–lined plate and season to taste with salt. Repeat with the remaining crab mixture, adding oil to the skillet as needed.

6 To serve, place the cooked crab cakes on a serving platter. Garnish with the remaining chives, sprinkle with salt, and serve with the lemon wedges and aioli.

QUEER EYE

Guacamole Cups

The Internet rebelled when Antoni Porowski, the food expert of *Queer Eye,* stirred a large spoonful of Greek yogurt into his homemade guacamole. Now, it may have been an unconventional choice, but we think Antoni's pairing of creamy, tangy yogurt with guac is an absolutely inspired makeover.

For this perfect-for-TV-watching appetizer, we make a garlicky yogurt crema to dollop on the bottom of our guacamole cups. The crema is topped with a classic guacamole, chopped tomato and radish, and a sprinkle of cilantro and pumpkin seeds.

YIELD: 30 guacamole cups   **PREP TIME:** 30 minutes   **COOK TIME:** 15 minutes    **VEGETARIAN**

YOGURT CREMA

2 limes

1 small garlic clove, finely chopped

¼ cup plain Greek yogurt

Pinch of chipotle chili powder or dark chili powder

1 teaspoon olive oil

1 teaspoon water

Kosher salt and freshly ground black pepper

GUACAMOLE

2 avocados

1 small white onion

1 small bunch fresh cilantro (about ½ ounce)

1 jalapeño, halved, seeded, and finely chopped

Kosher salt and freshly ground black pepper

1 medium tomato, cored and chopped

1 small radish, trimmed and chopped

30 tortilla chip cups

¼ cup roasted, salted shelled pumpkin seeds

1 **To make the yogurt crema:** Finely grate the zest of one lime, then juice both limes and set the juice aside. In a small bowl, combine the garlic, lime zest, Greek yogurt, chipotle chili powder or dark chili powder, olive oil, and water. Stir to combine. Season to taste with salt and pepper.

2 **To make the guacamole:** Finely chop 2 tablespoons of the onion (save the remaining onion for your own use). Finely chop the cilantro leaves and stems.

3 Halve the avocados, remove the pits, and scoop the flesh into a medium bowl. Coarsely mash the avocado with a fork. In the same bowl, add the onion, half of the chopped jalapeño, and 1 tablespoon of the lime juice. Stir to combine, then season to taste with salt and pepper. Add more lime juice, ½ teaspoon at a time if you want more acid, or more jalapeño for more spice. Stir in half of the chopped cilantro.

4 In a small bowl, combine the tomato and radish. Season with a pinch of salt.

5 **To assemble the guacamole cups:** Arrange the tortilla chip cups on a serving platter. Spoon a little yogurt crema at the bottom of each cup, then top with the guacamole. Garnish the cups with the tomato and radish, pumpkin seeds, and remaining cilantro.

Grace *and* Frankie

Watermelon Martini

A quick homemade watermelon juice makes this cocktail both colorful and refreshing. In the show *Grace and Frankie*, Grace's morning DIY version only required a whole watermelon and a bottle of vodka. But we added fresh lime juice, elderflower liqueur, and a pinch of salt to make this martini the best in town.

To create a delicious and nonalcoholic version, swap out the gin and elderflower liqueur with 4½ ounces of lemon-lime soda or seltzer.

YIELD: 2 cocktails
PREP TIME: 15 minutes

 VEGAN

12 ounces seedless watermelon, divided

1 lime

Pinch of kosher salt

3 ounces gin

1½ ounces elderflower liqueur

1 Cut the watermelon into 1-inch cubes. Set two cubes aside to use as a garnish.

2 In a small bowl, juice half of the lime (save the rest for your own use or thinly slice as a garnish).

3 Add the remaining melon and 1 teaspoon of the lime juice to a blender. Season with the salt. Puree until very smooth.

4 Place a fine-mesh strainer over a liquid measuring cup. Pour the watermelon juice through the strainer, pressing gently on the solids with a spoon. This should produce 6 ounces of watermelon juice. Taste the juice mixture, adding more lime juice if desired.

5 In a cocktail shaker, combine the watermelon juice, gin, and elderflower liqueur. Top with ice. Shake until the outside of the shaker feels cold, then strain into two martini glasses. Garnish with reserved watermelon cubes or a wedge of lime.

WATCH
GRACE AND FRANKIE

▶▶ Fast forward

Pro tip: The watermelon juice can be refrigerated in a sealed container for two days. This drink is equally delicious with store-bought fresh watermelon juice or you can skip the straining step for a slightly pulpier—dare we say healthier?—drink.

WATCH PARTY

STRANGER THINGS

Ready to watch—or rewatch—your favorite seasons as the group of friends from *Stranger Things* battle against the forces of evil? Gather your own friends and throw an epic viewing party with these entertaining décor suggestions, activity ideas, recipes, and more!

▶ **WATCH PARTY PLANNING**

WATCH PARTY PLANNING

Whether you're watching from the upside down or from the comfort of your own home, make it an adventure that you and your friends will never forget with these rad suggestions for décor, activities, recipes, and more!

▶ Setting the Scene

You may lure a Demogorgon to your party with your guest's laughter and excitement, so watch out!

- **Costume**: Ask your guests to show up dressed in their favorite '80s outfits. (Either outfits that you wore, or ones you can thrift.) Bonus points if you find a sweater just like Murray's!

- **Craft**: Create your own "Justice for Barb!" sign to hang and show your support.

- **Craft**: Hang up some colorful Christmas lights on a blank (or mostly blank) wall. Using masking tape, create an alphabet under the Christmas lights, resembling what Joyce made to communicate with Will. (This will come in handy later!)

- **Décor**: Make your own "Castle Byers" by creating a cozy, impenetrable blanket/pillow fort to watch your favorite episodes in.

- **Décor**: Add lots of sparkly or fun-colored D&D dice on the table to inspire your friends' RPG (Role Playing Game) campaigns.

▶ Pause & Play

- **Christmas Light Decoder**: Remember that Christmas light and tape alphabet display you created? Well, here's where it comes into play. Have one of your guests come up with any word and give the rest of the players hints as to how many letters the word is. Each player takes a turn guessing letters using the Christmas light decoder—almost like a weird game of hangman.

- **Walkie-Talkie Hide-and-Seek**: Find a few walkie-talkies for your guests and play a fun game of hide-and-seek. Just make sure to set safe boundaries if your game goes outside!

- **Triple-Decker Waffle Sundae Toppings Bar**: Buy a selection of toppings and have everyone customize their own waffle sundae.

- **Watch Party Drinking Game**: Take a drink of the delicious Watch Party cocktail (page 43) every time one of the mind-flayers shows up in an episode you are streaming.

- **Light as a Feather Game**: As Max says in the show "We make our own rules," so come up with your own variation of "Light as a Feather." Have each guest pretend they have telekinetic powers, like Eleven, and see what you can make move (or whom!) with this classic '80s sleepover game.

- **DIY RPG**: Create your own RPG characters either for a D&D campaign, a general one-shot RPG, or just for fun with the dice you put out on the table.

Strange Tuna Casserole

This is the perfect retro classic for a *Stranger Things* watch party. Our creamy, cheesy mini casseroles are topped with cheddar cheese and a generous cap of crushed potato chips. The recipe calls for two snack-sized bags of chips, but if you need more to get you through the scarier scenes, we think everyone would approve.

YIELD: 12 mini casseroles   **PREP TIME:** 15 minutes   **COOK TIME:** 40 minutes

Unsalted butter or cooking spray for greasing

Kosher salt

4 ounces egg noodles (about 2½ cups)

½ cup frozen peas

One 10½-ounce can cream of mushroom soup

¼ cup sour cream

¼ cup heavy cream or milk

1 large egg

1 teaspoon Dijon mustard

Freshly ground black pepper

1 red or yellow bell pepper, finely chopped

2 scallions, thinly sliced

Two 5-ounce cans light tuna packed in water, drained

1¼ cups grated sharp cheddar cheese

1 small bunch fresh Italian parsley (about ½ ounce), chopped

Two 1-ounce bags potato chips

1. Lightly grease a 12-cup muffin pan with the butter or cooking spray. Preheat the oven to 350°F/177°C with a rack in the center position. Bring a medium pot of salted water to a boil. Add the egg noodles to the pot and cook according to package directions. Two minutes before the noodles finish cooking, add the peas. Drain the noodles and peas.

2. In a large bowl, combine the soup, sour cream, heavy cream or milk, egg, and mustard. Season with ¼ teaspoon salt and a few grinds of pepper. Whisk until smooth.

3. Finely chop the parsley leaves and stems. Add the noodles, peas, pepper, scallions, tuna, ¾ cup of the cheddar, and half of the parsley to the same bowl, then stir to combine. Divide the tuna noodle mixture among the muffin cups.

4. Lightly crush the potato chips, then top the mini casseroles with the chips and the remaining ½ cup of cheddar.

5. Transfer the mini casseroles to the oven and bake for 25 to 30 minutes, until golden brown on top and bubbling around the edges. Let cool for 5 minutes.

6. To serve, run a small knife around the edge of each cup to loosen it. Transfer the mini casseroles to a serving platter and garnish with the remaining parsley.

Mini Meat Loaves Topped with Mashed Potatoes

Baking these mini meat loaves in muffin tins speeds up the cooking, and the portion is perfect for a watch party. For the mashed potato topping, you can either use a pastry bag and piping tip of your choice or dollop the mashed potatoes on top with a spoon.

YIELD: 12 mini meat loaves
PREP TIME: 15 minutes
COOK TIME: 1 hour

WATCH
STRANGER THINGS

NETFLIX

MINI MEAT LOAVES

1 tablespoon vegetable oil, plus more for greasing

1 small yellow onion, finely chopped

1 garlic clove, finely chopped

1 large egg

1 tablespoon Worcestershire sauce

1 tablespoon plus 2 teaspoons spicy brown or Dijon mustard, divided

¼ cup ketchup, divided

1 small bunch fresh parsley (about ½ ounce), finely chopped

1 pound ground beef

¼ cup panko bread crumbs

1 teaspoon kosher salt

¼ teaspoon freshly ground black pepper

MASHED POTATOES

4 Yukon Gold potatoes (about 1 pound)

Kosher salt

2 tablespoons sour cream

2 tablespoons unsalted butter

¾ cup shredded sharp cheddar cheese

1 small bunch fresh chives (about ¼ ounce), thinly sliced

Freshly ground black pepper

1 **To make the meat loaves:** Preheat the oven to 375°F/190°C with a rack in the center position. Lightly grease a 12-cup muffin tin. In a medium skillet, heat the vegetable oil over medium-high. Transfer the onion and garlic to the skillet, then cook for 2 to 3 minutes, until softened. Scrape the onion and garlic mixture into a small bowl and cool slightly.

2 In a medium bowl, combine the egg, Worcestershire sauce, 2 teaspoons of the mustard, and 2 tablespoons of the ketchup. To the same bowl, add the chopped parsley, cooled onion and garlic mixture, ground beef, bread crumbs, salt, and pepper. Mix with your hands to combine.

3 Divide the meat loaf mixture among the prepared muffin tin cups. In a small bowl, combine the remaining 2 tablespoons of ketchup and 1 tablespoon of mustard, then spoon over the meat loaves. Transfer to the center rack of the oven and bake for about 15 minutes, until the meat loaves are cooked through and browned on top.

4 **To make the mashed potatoes:** While the meat loaves bake, scrub the potatoes, then peel and cut them into 1-inch chunks. Place in a medium saucepan and add salted water to cover about 1 inch. Cover the saucepan and bring to a boil over high heat. Uncover, reduce the heat to medium-high, then cook for about 8 minutes, until the potatoes can be easily pierced with a fork. Drain the potatoes, then return to the saucepan.

5 Add the sour cream, butter, ½ cup of the cheddar cheese, and half of the chives to the pot with the potatoes, then mash well to combine. Season to taste with salt and pepper.

6 Spoon some of the mashed potatoes over each meat loaf (Or use a pastry bag fitted with the tip of your choice if you're feeling fancy!). Sprinkle with the remaining ¼ cup of cheese.

7 Return to the oven and bake for 5 to 7 minutes, until the potatoes are lightly browned on top and the cheese has melted. Garnish with the remaining chives before serving.

Triple-Decker Waffle Sundaes

These triple-decker waffle sundaes might be the ultimate viewing-party food—indulgent, pretty easy to make, and totally delicious. We make our layers with crunchy DIY honey-roasted peanuts, a quick chocolate sauce, and plenty of tangy whipped cream. Make sure to save enough chocolate coated candies and chocolate sauce to make your own Christmas light decorations on top!

YIELD: 4 waffle sundaes
PREP TIME: 10 minutes
COOK TIME: 30 minutes

🌿 VEGETARIAN

🥜 CONTAINS NUTS

2 tablespoons honey

1 cup roasted salted peanuts
(optional, if nut allergy exists)

Kosher salt

4 ounces bittersweet chocolate,
finely chopped

2¾ cups heavy cream, divided

½ cup sour cream

2 tablespoons confectioners'
sugar

12 frozen waffles, preferably
Eggo (Eleven's favorite)

Mini, peanut, or regular chocolate
coated candies for serving

▶▶ Fast forward

Homemade whipped cream
always feels special and
tastes even more delicious.
A few tips for making the
very best homemade version:

Cold is key: Remove the
heavy cream and sour
cream from the fridge just
before whipping.

What is a soft peak? When
you lift the whisk up and
then flip it upside down, the
cream will fall into a softly
curved peak.

**Whipped cream can be
made ahead of time and
refrigerated for up to 8
hours;** simply re-whip a bit
before serving.

1 Preheat the oven to 350°F/177°C with a rack in the center position.
Line a rimmed baking sheet with parchment paper.

2 Add the honey to a medium microwave-safe bowl. Microwave on
high for about 30 seconds, until the honey is runny. Add the peanuts
to the bowl with the honey and stir to coat. Season with a pinch of salt.

3 Transfer the honey-coated peanuts to the oven. (Wash the bowl for
step 4.) Bake for about 12 minutes, until the peanuts are toasted and
the honey has started to caramelize. Remove the peanuts from the oven
and cool completely. Increase the oven temperature to 450°F/230°C.

4 Add the chocolate to the reserved clean bowl. In a small saucepan,
heat ¾ cup of the heavy cream over low for about 2 minutes, until it's
just beginning to steam and simmer. Carefully pour the cream over the
chopped chocolate and let stand at room temperature for about 5 minutes,
until the chocolate begins to melt. Season the chocolate sauce with a
pinch of salt and whisk until smooth. Cover and keep warm. Alternatively,
heat the cream in a medium microwave-safe bowl for 45 seconds to
1 minute, until just steaming. Add the chocolate to the bowl, then let
stand for 5 minutes. Then proceed with the recipe.

5 In a large bowl (or in a mixer bowl fitted with the whisk attachment),
combine the remaining 2 cups of cream, sour cream, and sugar.
Whisk until the cream holds soft peaks.

6 Coarsely chop the cooled peanuts, if desired, then transfer to a plate.
Discard the parchment paper from the baking sheet. On the same
baking sheet, arrange the waffles in a single layer. Transfer to the oven
and bake for 5 to 7 minutes, until crispy and hot. Let cool slightly.

7 To assemble, spoon some of the whipped cream on one waffle,
then sprinkle with some of the peanuts, chocolate coated candies, and
then drizzle with a little chocolate sauce. Repeat with a second waffle,
peanuts, chocolate coated candies, and chocolate sauce. Top with the
third waffle and spoon more whipped cream on top. Drizzle a little chocolate sauce in a swooping line over the top, then add some chocolate
coated candies to mimic the Christmas lights that Joyce hangs up in her
living room in the first season. Repeat with the remaining
ingredients to make three more sundaes.

Ginger & Molasses Pineapple Upside-Down Cake

The perfect dark dessert for a *Stranger Things* watch party or marathon might just be a Ginger & Molasses Pineapple Upside-Down Cake. This classic cake with sunny pineapple rings and bright red cherries on top hides a darker cake layer just below.

Pineapple upside-down cakes often have a yellow cake base, but we think the ginger-molasses cake balances the sweetness of the pineapple topping. A splash of rum in the pineapple topping is delicious, but definitely optional.

YIELD: One 9-inch cake   **PREP TIME:** 20 minutes
COOK TIME: 1 hour, plus cooling

 VEGETARIAN

1 **To make the topping:** Preheat the oven to 350°F/177°C with a rack in the center position. Drain the pineapple rings, then pat dry. In a 10-inch cast-iron or ovenproof skillet, melt the butter over medium heat for about 3 minutes. Add 3 tablespoons of the melted butter to a small bowl and reserve for step 4.

2 To the same skillet over medium heat, stir in the brown sugar, rum (if desired), ginger, and salt, whisking for about 2 minutes, until the sugar dissolves and the liquid has reduced slightly. Remove the skillet from the heat. Carefully arrange the pineapple rings on top of the brown sugar mixture, placing a cherry in the center of each ring. Use cut-up pieces of pineapple to fill in the gaps.

3 **To make the cake:** In a medium bowl, thoroughly combine the flour, salt, ginger, baking soda, baking powder, cinnamon, cloves, and nutmeg.

4 To a large bowl, add the molasses, egg, granulated sugar, sour cream, milk, and reserved 3 tablespoons of butter, then whisk until combined. Add the dry ingredients, then stir with a spatula until just combined. Pour the batter over the pineapple topping, smoothing the top of the batter with a spatula.

5 Transfer to the center rack of the oven. Bake for about 35 minutes, until the cake springs back lightly to the touch and a cake tester or toothpick inserted into the center comes out with a few moist crumbs.

6 Let the cake cool for 5 minutes, then carefully invert it onto a large plate or cake stand. Leave the skillet in place for 30 seconds, then carefully remove it. Any fruit or caramel still in the skillet can be put back on top of the cake. Cool completely for about 30 minutes before serving. Serve with a dollop of whipped cream if desired.

TOPPING

One 20-ounce can pineapple rings in juice

7 tablespoons unsalted butter, divided

½ cup light brown sugar

1 teaspoon dark rum (optional)

¼ teaspoon ground ginger

¼ teaspoon kosher salt

12 maraschino cherries, or 6 fresh bing cherries, halved and pitted

CAKE

1¾ cups all-purpose flour

1 teaspoon kosher salt

1½ teaspoons ground ginger

¾ teaspoon baking soda

½ teaspoon baking powder

1 teaspoon ground cinnamon

¼ teaspoon ground cloves

¼ teaspoon ground nutmeg

¾ cup molasses

1 large egg

¼ cup granulated sugar

⅓ cup sour cream

¼ cup milk

Whipped cream for serving (optional)

WATCH
STRANGER THINGS

The Watch Party Cocktail

To round out our *Stranger Things* watch party with a drink pairing, we recommend a cocktail as dark and twisted as evil itself. This dramatic drink combines muddled blackberries and lime on the bottom of the glass with a mist of sparkling wine on top.

To make a mocktail version, use white grape or apple juice in place of both the white wine and berry liqueur, and either berry seltzer or a lemon-lime soda instead of the sparkling wine.

YIELD: 4 cocktails
PREP TIME: 5 minutes

 VEGAN

2 teaspoons granulated sugar

1 cup blackberries, plus more for garnishing

Juice of 1 lime

3 ounces berry liqueur

2 ounces white wine

Chilled sparkling wine for serving

1 In a cocktail shaker, combine the sugar, 1 cup of blackberries, lime juice, and berry liqueur. Using a muddler or a spoon, crush the blackberry mixture into a thick pulp. Add the white wine to the shaker, then fill the shaker halfway with ice. Shake for about 30 seconds, until the outside of the shaker feels cool.

2 Strain the blackberry mixture into a liquid measuring cup, then divide among four champagne flutes. Top with sparkling wine and garnish with a few blackberries.

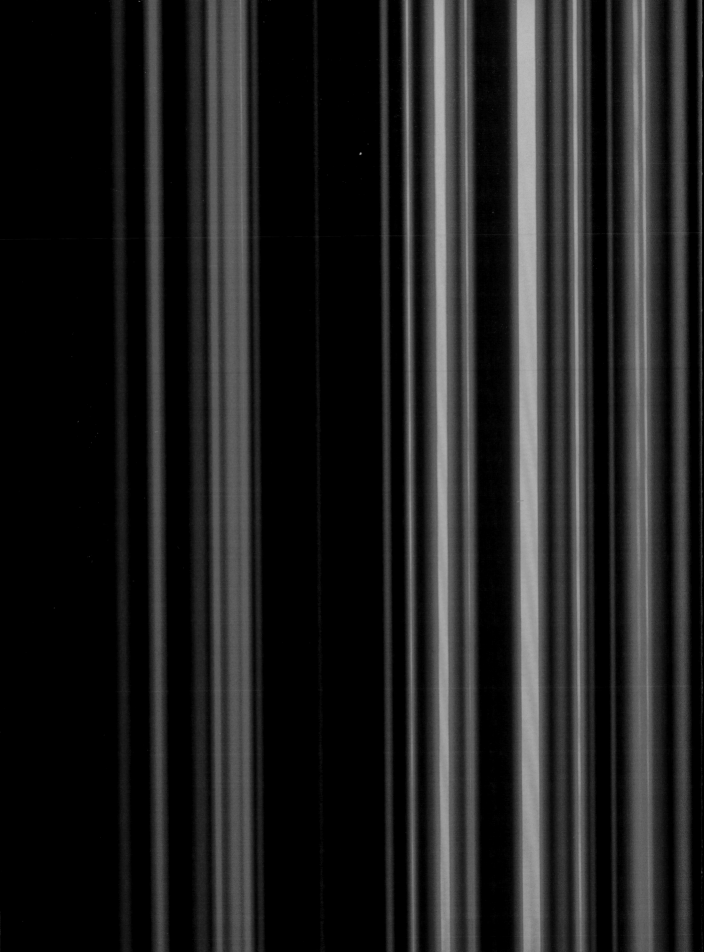

Host Your Own Food Show

Have you ever watched a cooking show and thought, "I could do that"? Here's your chance! Let's dive into eleven delicious recipes with no pesky time limits or judging.

SALT FAT ACID HEAT

Buttermilk Chicken Sandwich

On her show *Salt Fat Acid Heat,* Samin Nosrat teams up with collaborator and illustrator Wendy MacNaughton to cook her famous buttermilk roast chicken as part of a dinner party. For the party, Samin pairs the chicken with a salad that contains creamy white beans, roasted vegetables, a punchy shallot vinaigrette, crumbled feta cheese, and lots of herbs.

Inspired by this menu, we created a sandwich that uses salt, fat, acid, and, yes, heat. Instead of roasting a whole chicken, we marinate two bone-in chicken breasts in buttermilk and salt, then roast until juicy and tender. Bite-sized pieces of chicken are piled on toasted ciabatta rolls that are slathered with a creamy feta spread and topped with both soft roasted tomatoes and a crunchy, bright celery and herb salad.

YIELD: 4 sandwiches
PREP TIME: 30 minutes, plus marinating and resting
COOK TIME: 1 hour

BUTTERMILK CHICKEN

2 bone-in, skin-on chicken breasts (about 2 pounds)

Kosher salt

1 cup buttermilk

Freshly ground black pepper

ROASTED TOMATOES

3 plum or Campari tomatoes

2 sprigs fresh thyme

1 tablespoon olive oil

Kosher salt and freshly ground black pepper

CREAMY FETA SPREAD

4 ounces feta, crumbled

1 garlic clove, peeled and finely grated

½ cup labneh

Kosher salt and freshly ground black pepper

2 tablespoons water

2 tablespoons olive oil

1 tablespoon za'atar

CELERY AND HERB SALAD

1 shallot, peeled

2 teaspoons red wine vinegar

Kosher salt and freshly ground black pepper

2 tablespoons olive oil

2 stalks celery, thinly sliced

1 small bunch fresh parsley (about ½ ounce), coarsely chopped

1 small bunch fresh dill (about ½ ounce), coarsely chopped

4 ciabatta rolls, halved

Olive oil for drizzling

1 garlic clove, peeled

1 **To prepare the chicken:** Pat the chicken breasts dry, then season generously all over with salt. Let stand at room temperature for 30 minutes. In a liquid measuring cup, combine the buttermilk and 1 tablespoon of salt. Transfer the chicken to a large resealable plastic bag, then pour the buttermilk over the top. Press as much air out of the bag as possible, then seal. Gently squeeze the bag to help coat the chicken in the buttermilk. Refrigerate the marinated chicken overnight.

2 **To roast the chicken and tomatoes:** Remove the chicken from the refrigerator 1 hour before cooking. Preheat the oven to 450°F/232°C with racks in the center and lower third positions. Line a rimmed baking sheet with parchment paper. Core the tomatoes, then cut lengthwise into ½-inch slices. Place the tomatoes and thyme sprigs on the baking sheet. Drizzle the tomatoes with the olive oil, then season with salt and pepper. Remove the chicken breasts from the marinade, shaking off as much of the buttermilk as possible, and transfer to a medium ovenproof skillet.

3 Roast the chicken on the center rack for about 30 minutes, until the chicken skin is deeply browned and the meat is cooked through. Roast the tomatoes on the lower rack for about 30 minutes, until very soft and charred in spots. Remove both the tomatoes and chicken from the oven. Let stand at room temperature for 10 to 15 minutes, until cool enough to touch.

4 **To make the feta spread:** To a medium bowl, add the feta, garlic, labneh, and a pinch each of salt and pepper, then mash the ingredients with a fork to combine. Add the water and olive oil to the bowl, and stir to combine. The feta mixture should be spreadable, so add extra olive oil and water, 1 teaspoon at a time, to achieve the desired consistency. Stir in the za'atar.

5 **To assemble the celery and herb salad:** Thinly slice the shallot crosswise, and place it in a medium bowl. Toss the shallot with the vinegar and a pinch each of salt and pepper. Let marinate for 10 minutes. Stir the olive oil into the marinated shallots, then add the celery, parsley, and dill to the same bowl. Toss to combine, then season to taste with salt and pepper.

6 **To assemble the sandwiches:** Preheat the broiler with a rack 6 inches from the heat source. Drizzle the rolls with olive oil. Broil the rolls, cut side up, for 1 to 2 minutes, until lightly toasted (watch closely as broilers vary). Rub the cut sides of the rolls with the garlic clove.

7 Remove the breast meat and skin from the cooled chicken, then tear the meat into bite-sized pieces. Slather the feta spread on the cut sides of the rolls, then top four halves with the roasted tomatoes, chicken, and celery and herb salad. Top with the remaining roll halves.

"Salt, fat, acid, heat—just four basic elements that can make or break a dish."

—SAMIN NOSRAT

Cod and Clam Chowder

On the season finale of *The Final Table*, four contestants have two hours to create a dish that will earn them a place with the nine iconic culinary judges—a dish, as host Andrew Knowlton says, "that will create a legend." Season one winner Chef Timothy Hollingsworth presents the chef judges a dish of black cod, razor and littleneck clams, potato mousseline, leek ash, and burnt alliums—a recipe that he made famous at his restaurant, Otium.

Inspired by Chef Hollingsworth's prize-winning, chowder-inspired plate, we created this restaurant-worthy bowl of sublime clam and cod chowder. By cooking the clams separately, you are able to make your own clam broth, rather than relying on premade broth or clam juice. And while chowder is often served with oyster crackers, here we make our own buttery croutons with a hint of Old Bay seasoning to top our chowder. These homemade touches will bring a *Final Table* flourish to this delicious meal.

YIELD: 4 servings **PREP TIME:** 2 hours **COOK TIME:** 1 hour

3 pounds littleneck clams

3 slices sourdough or peasant bread (about ½ inch thick)

2 tablespoons vegetable oil

4 tablespoons unsalted butter, divided

Kosher salt and freshly ground black pepper

½ teaspoon Old Bay seasoning

1 large leek

3 medium Yukon Gold potatoes (about 1½ pounds)

2 sprigs fresh thyme

1 bay leaf

2 garlic cloves, peeled

1 yellow onion, peeled and finely chopped

⅓ cup white wine or dry vermouth (optional)

3 stalks celery, thinly sliced

1½ pounds cod filets

1¼ cups heavy cream

1 lemon

1 small bunch fresh parsley (about ½ ounce), finely chopped

1 In a large bowl, cover the clams with cold water. Let stand at room temperature for 20 minutes. Lift the clams out of the water, then place them in a colander. Discard the sandy water, then rinse the bowl. Return the clams to the same bowl, cover them with clean water, and repeat the process, changing the water about every 20 minutes, until no grit or sand remains. (This should take about 1 hour.)

2 While the clams soak, tear the bread into 1-inch pieces. In a large skillet, heat the oil and 2 tablespoons of the butter over medium for about 2 minutes, until the butter melts. Add the torn bread to the same skillet, then season with a pinch each of salt and pepper. Cook, stirring occasionally, for 5 to 7 minutes, until the bread is golden brown and crispy. Sprinkle the croutons with the Old Bay seasoning, then cook for about 30 seconds, until the spice is fragrant. Transfer the croutons to a plate, then let set at room temperature.

3 Trim off the dark green portion of the leek and discard, then halve the leek lengthwise. Thinly slice each leek half crosswise into half-moons. Add the sliced leeks to a medium bowl, then cover with cold water. Swish the leeks with your fingers to loosen any dirt or grit, then lift the leeks out of the bowl and transfer to a plate. Rinse the bowl, then fill it with clean cold water. Scrub the potatoes, then cut into ¾-inch pieces and transfer to the bowl with cold water.

>>recipe continues on the next page

WATCH
THE FINAL TABLE

>>Cod and Clam Chowder continued

4 To a large pot, add the cleaned clams, thyme, bay leaf, and 4½ cups of cold water. Crush one garlic clove and finely chop the other. Add the crushed clove to the pot with the clams. Over medium heat, bring the clams and the cooking liquid to a simmer, then cover and cook for 5 to 10 minutes, until the clams open. Remove the pot from the heat.

5 Using a slotted spoon, transfer the opened clams to a large bowl. (Discard any clams that have not opened.) Pour the cooking liquid through a fine-mesh strainer into a medium bowl or large heatproof measuring cup, then discard the aromatics. (You should have about 4 cups of liquid.) Save one-third of the clams in their shells for serving, then remove the remaining clam meat from the shells and cut into ½-inch pieces.

6 Wipe out the pot, then return to the stove top and add the remaining 2 tablespoons of butter. Heat the butter over medium until melted, then add the chopped garlic, onion, and leeks. Season with salt and pepper, then cook for 5 to 6 minutes, until softened. Add the wine or vermouth, if desired, then cook for about 2 minutes, until the liquid has nearly evaporated.

7 To the same pot, add the celery, potatoes, and clam liquid, then bring to a boil over high heat. Reduce the heat to medium, then cook for about 12 minutes, until the potatoes are tender.

8 Meanwhile, pat the cod dry, then cut it into 2-inch pieces. Once the potatoes are tender, crush some of the potatoes with a spoon to thicken the soup. To the same pot, add the cooked clams, cod, and heavy cream. Simmer over medium heat for 2 to 3 minutes, until the cod is opaque and the clams are warm. Remove the pot from the heat, then season the broth to taste with salt and pepper.

9 Finely grate the zest from half of the lemon, then stir it into the chowder. Add half of the parsley to the chowder.

10 Divide the chowder among four bowls, then garnish with the croutons and the remaining parsley.

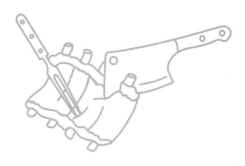

UGLY DELICIOUS

Braised Short Ribs

4 pounds beef short ribs, cut crosswise into 2- to 3-inch pieces

2 medium red onions

1 small Asian pear, peeled

¾ cup soy sauce

¼ cup light brown sugar

¼ cup honey

½ cup mirin

½ cup red wine (for a nonalcoholic version, use apple juice)

1 tablespoon toasted sesame oil

Kosher salt and freshly ground black pepper

Vegetable oil for cooking

5 garlic cloves, crushed

1-inch piece fresh ginger, peeled and thinly sliced

2 cups low-sodium chicken broth

3 to 4 carrots (about 12 ounces)

3 Yukon Gold potatoes (about 12 ounces)

1 medium daikon radish (about 12 ounces)

2 cups jasmine rice

2 cups water

1 teaspoon kosher salt

4 scallions, thinly sliced

½ cup pine nuts

In the home cooking–themed episode of his show *Ugly Delicious*, Chef David Chang makes his wife galbi jjim, a short rib stew. Then he and his friend Peter Meehan travel to Virginia to help cook the Chang family's Thanksgiving dinner. As David and his mom, Sherri, shop at the local H Mart after his arrival, she firmly reminds him that rice cakes do *not* go in galbi jjim.

Our galbi jjim–inspired braised short ribs have a rich, sweet, and savory sauce, but instead of rice cakes, we use tender chunks of potatoes, carrots, and daikon radish. Serve the braised meat over steamed rice with scallions and pine nuts sprinkled over the top.

YIELD: 4 servings
PREP TIME: 40 minutes, plus 30 minutes soaking
COOK TIME: 4 hours

 CONTAINS NUTS

1 In a large bowl of cold water, soak the short ribs for 30 minutes. Drain in a colander, then rinse with cold water.

2 Fill a medium pot halfway with water, then bring to a boil. Transfer the short ribs to the boiling water and blanch for 5 minutes. Drain the short ribs, then repeat the blanching process two more times and then pat the short ribs very dry.

3 While the short ribs are blanching, peel and halve the onions. Cut each half into 1-inch wedges, leaving the root end intact. Coarsely grate the pear on the large holes of a box grater. (This should yield about ¾ cup.)

4 In a medium bowl, combine the soy sauce, brown sugar, honey, mirin, red wine, sesame oil, and grated pear, whisking until the sugar is dissolved. Set this braising liquid aside for step 7.

5 Preheat the oven to 400°F/204°C with a rack in the center position. Season the short ribs all over with salt and pepper. In a large Dutch oven, heat 1 tablespoon vegetable oil over medium-high. Working in batches, transfer the short ribs to the Dutch oven, being careful not to crowd the pot. Cook the short ribs, turning occasionally, for 10 to 12 minutes, until browned on all sides. Transfer to a plate. Repeat with the remaining short ribs, adding more oil, 1 tablespoon at a time, as needed.

>>recipe continues on the next page

▶▶ Fast forward

If you plan to serve the short ribs the next day, after step 10, use a slotted spoon to remove the short ribs and vegetables, then store the liquid and the short ribs and vegetables separately. Before serving, remove the short ribs from the bones, then combine the now-boneless short ribs, vegetables, and braising liquid. Heat over medium, seasoning to taste with salt and pepper before serving.

>>Braised Short Ribs continued

6 Once the short ribs have all browned, put 1 tablespoon of oil and the onions, garlic, and ginger into the Dutch oven. Reduce the heat to medium. Cook for 5 to 7 minutes, stirring and scraping any browned bits off the bottom, until the onions are just tender.

7 Return the short ribs and any juices to the Dutch oven. Add the reserved braising liquid and the chicken broth. Increase the heat to medium-high, then bring the liquid to a boil. Remove the Dutch oven from the heat. Transfer to the oven and braise for about 1 hour, until the short ribs are nearly tender.

8 Meanwhile, scrub the carrots, potatoes, and radish. Peel the carrots and the daikon, then cut them into 1-inch chunks. Cut the potatoes into 1-inch pieces.

9 Remove the short ribs from the oven. Reduce the heat to 350°F/ 177°C. Uncover and stir in the carrots, potatoes, and radish. Return to the oven and cook for about 1 hour, until the short ribs and vegetables are very tender.

10 Using a slotted spoon, transfer the short ribs and vegetables to a large plate and cover to keep warm. Discard the garlic and ginger. Bring the braising liquid to a boil, then reduce the heat to medium-high. Cook for about 10 minutes, until the sauce has reduced slightly and is just thick enough to coat the back of a spoon. Season the liquid to taste with salt and pepper. Discard the bones from the short ribs, if desired, then return the meat and vegetables to the liquid. Cover to keep warm.

11 In a medium saucepan, combine the rice, water, and salt. Bring to a boil, then cover, reduce the heat to low, and cook for 17 minutes. Remove the pan from the heat and let the rice stand for 5 minutes. Remove the lid and fluff the rice with a fork.

12 Serve the braised short ribs, vegetables, and braising liquid with the rice. Garnish with the scallions and pine nuts.

NETFLIX

WATCH
UGLY DELICIOUS

FRESH FRIED AND CRISPY

St. Louis Toasted Ravioli

Also known as T-Rav, toasted ravioli is a signature St. Louis dish. When *Fresh, Fried and Crispy* visited the city, host Daym Drops tries the toasted beef ravioli made by Zia's on the Hill's Nick Chiodini. Nick fried up beef ravioli for Daym, but you can use whatever fresh ravioli flavor you like best.

While Zia's uses commercial deep-fry equipment, you can achieve restaurant-quality results with a large Dutch oven and a deep-fry thermometer. A few pro tips: Don't fry too many ravioli at once. The temperature of the oil will drop too much, and the ravioli will cook more slowly and end up oilier. Also, make sure you let the oil come back up to temperature before adding the next batch. Frying each batch at the correct temperature will help you make the deeply browned T-Ravs that Daym loved so much.

YIELD: 4 appetizer servings   **PREP TIME:** 30 minutes, plus chilling   **COOK TIME:** 35 minutes

1 ounce Parmigiano Reggiano, divided

1 pound fresh ravioli

½ cup all-purpose flour

1 large egg

Kosher salt and freshly ground black pepper

1 cup dry bread crumbs

1½ teaspoons Italian seasoning

½ teaspoon garlic powder

Vegetable oil for frying

2 cups marinara sauce

1 small bunch fresh basil (about ½ ounce) (optional)

1   Finely grate the Parmigiano Reggiano (you should have about ¾ cup grated cheese). Remove the ravioli from the packaging, carefully separating the pieces if necessary. Line a rimmed baking sheet with parchment paper.

2   Add the flour to a medium wide bowl or pie plate. In a medium shallow bowl, lightly beat the egg, then season with a pinch each of salt and pepper. In a third medium bowl, add the bread crumbs, Italian seasoning, garlic powder, and ⅔ cup of the Parmigiano.

3   Working a few pieces at a time, toss the ravioli in the flour, then transfer to the egg mixture. Lift the ravioli out of the egg one at a time, letting the excess drip back into the bowl. Transfer to the bread crumb mixture, patting gently to help the bread crumbs adhere. Place the breaded ravioli on the prepared baking sheet. Repeat with the remaining ravioli, then place in the freezer for at least 15 minutes to firm up while you heat the oil.

4   In a large Dutch oven, heat 2 inches of vegetable oil to 350°F/177°C over medium-high. Set a wire cooling rack over a rimmed baking sheet or line a baking tray with paper towels.

5   Working in batches, transfer the breaded ravioli to the hot oil, then fry for 2 to 3 minutes per side, until puffed and golden brown. Transfer the ravioli to the prepared baking sheet or tray, and season with salt. Allow the oil to come back to 350°F/177°C before adding more ravioli.

6   While the ravioli is frying, heat the marinara in a small saucepan over medium-low until just warm.

7   To serve, garnish with the remaining 2 tablespoons Parmigiano and some thinly sliced basil, if desired. Serve with the warm marinara sauce on the side for dipping.

TACO CHRONICLES

The Fish Taco Chronicles

In *Taco Chronicles*, the rich and varied histories of different taco styles are explored through the lens of both the chefs who cook them and the customers who are passionate about them. In the seventh episode of the second season, taco de pescado goes under the culinary microscope. Viewers learn about the different regional styles of this taco and the Japanese influence on the type of batter used.

We put our new taco knowledge to use to prepare truly delicious fish tacos. There are classic toppings—thinly shredded cabbage, salsa Mexicana, mayonnaise, limes, and hot sauce—plus fresh fish fried in a light tempura-style beer batter.

YIELD: 12 tacos   **PREP TIME:** 20 minutes   **COOK TIME:** 45 minutes

1 small head green cabbage (about 8 ounces)

3 medium tomatoes, cored and finely chopped

1 small white onion, finely chopped

1 small bunch fresh cilantro (about 1 ounce), finely chopped

2 limes, cut into wedges

Kosher salt and freshly ground black pepper

½ cup mayonnaise

¼ teaspoon chipotle chili powder

1½ pounds firm white fish, such as cod, pollock, or mahi-mahi

1½ cups all-purpose flour, divided

1 cup light beer

Vegetable oil for frying

12 (6-inch) corn tortillas

Pickled jalapeños for serving (optional)

Mexican hot sauce for serving (optional)

1 Very thinly slice 3 cups of cabbage (save the remaining cabbage for your own use).

2 In a medium bowl, combine the tomatoes, onion, and half of the cilantro. Season this salsa Mexicana with salt and the juice of 2 lime wedges. Stir to combine. In a small bowl, combine the mayonnaise and chipotle chili powder, and season with a pinch each of salt and pepper.

3 Pat the fish dry, then cut into strips about 1 inch wide and 4 inches long. Transfer ½ cup of the flour to a plate. Set aside. In a shallow medium bowl, whisk to combine the remaining 1 cup of flour, 1 teaspoon of salt, and a few grinds of pepper. In a slow, steady stream, whisk the beer into the dry ingredients until barely combined. (Do not overmix.)

4 In a large Dutch oven, heat 2 inches of vegetable oil to 350°F/177°C. Place a wire rack over a rimmed baking sheet.

5 While the oil is heating, place a medium cast-iron skillet over high heat. Working in batches, transfer the corn tortillas to the skillet, then cook for about 30 seconds per side, until warm, pliable, and browned in a few spots. Wrap the warm tortillas in foil, then repeat with the remaining tortillas.

6 When the oil reaches 350°F/177°C, sprinkle the fish pieces with salt. Working with 4 to 5 fish pieces at a time, transfer them to the plate, then lightly dust with the flour, shaking off the excess. Lift the fish out of the flour and add them to the batter. Lift the fish out of the batter, letting the excess batter drip back into the bowl. Transfer the fish to the hot oil. Cook, turning once, for 1 to 2 minutes per side, until the batter is puffed and golden brown. Remove to the wire rack and season with salt. Repeat with the remaining fish and batter.

7 Build the tacos at the table with the fried fish, warm tortillas, cabbage, salsa Mexicana, and chipotle mayonnaise. Squeeze the lime wedges over the top, then add pickled jalapeños or hot sauce if desired.

Miami Cuban Sandwich

"A Cuban sandwich is like an explosion of flavors in your mouth," says Melissa Elias of Luis Galindo's, which was featured in *Street Food: Miami.* The Cuban sandwiches at Luis Galindo's are deliciously made with roast pork shoulder, sweet sliced ham, Swiss cheese, yellow mustard, and sour pickles, pressed on generously buttered bread.

For our version, we use a mojo-marinated pork tenderloin in place of the classic roast pork, which requires a longer roasting time. We also show you how to create a DIY sandwich press out of two skillets. Beyond that, the ham is sweet, the pickles are sour, both butter and mustard are generously applied, and the melted Swiss holds everything together. We love the herby, garlicky flavor that chimichurri adds to the sandwich, but it's definitely optional.

YIELD: 4 sandwiches
PREP TIME: 15 minutes, plus 30 minutes marinating
COOK TIME: 1 hour

WATCH
STREET FOOD USA

ROAST PORK

2 large garlic cloves, finely grated

⅓ cup of freshly squeezed orange juice

2 tablespoons of freshly squeezed lime juice

¼ cup olive oil

1 teaspoon kosher salt

1 teaspoon dried oregano

½ teaspoon ground cumin

½ teaspoon freshly ground black pepper

1 pound pork tenderloin

4 Cuban sandwich rolls or hero rolls, 8 to 10 inches long

4 sour dill pickles, plus more for serving

4 tablespoons unsalted butter, softened

½ cup yellow mustard

¼ cup chimichurri (optional)

1 pound thinly sliced deli ham

8 ounces thinly sliced Swiss cheese

Vegetable oil for cooking

1 **To make the roast pork:** To a medium shallow bowl, add the garlic, orange juice, lime juice, olive oil, salt, oregano, cumin, and pepper; whisk to combine. Pat the pork tenderloin dry, then add to the marinade, turning to coat. Cover with plastic wrap and marinate at room temperature for 30 minutes.

2 Preheat the oven to 375°F/190°C with a rack in the center position. Line a rimmed baking sheet with aluminum foil. Place the pork tenderloin on the prepared baking sheet, spooning the marinade over the top. Transfer the pork tenderloin to the oven and roast for about 30 minutes, until an instant-read thermometer inserted into the thickest part is at 140°F/60°C.

3 Remove the tenderloin from the oven, place on a cutting board, and tent with aluminum foil. Let rest for 10 minutes, then thinly slice on an angle.

4 **To assemble the sandwiches:** Split the sandwich rolls in half lengthwise. Slice 4 pickles lengthwise. Spread 1 tablespoon of the softened butter on the outside of each piece of roll. Arrange, buttered side down, on a clean work surface. Spread 1 tablespoon of mustard on the cut side of each piece of roll. Spread 1 tablespoon of the chimichurri over the mustard, if desired. Divide the sliced ham evenly among four halves of the bread, then top with the pickles. Add the sliced roast pork, spooning any juices from the cutting board over the top. Top the roast pork with the Swiss cheese, then close up the sandwiches.

5 Wrap the bottom of a large heavy skillet in aluminum foil. Drizzle a little vegetable oil in a second large skillet, then heat over medium. Transfer two of the sandwiches to the skillet, then press down with the foil-wrapped skillet. Cook for about 5 minutes, until the sandwiches are golden brown on the bottom. Flip over, press down again, and continue to cook for about 5 minutes more, until the second side is golden brown and the cheese has melted. Repeat with the two remaining sandwiches. Cut the sandwiches in half and serve with extra pickles on the side.

"The best food is on the street: incredibly rich, diverse, bursting with flavor."

—SHOW OPENER

HIGH ON THE HOG

HOW AFRICAN AMERICAN CUISINE
TRANSFORMED AMERICA

Baked Mac & Cheese with Virginia Ham

In the third episode of *High on the Hog*, host Stephen Satterfield travels to Monticello in Virginia to learn about enslaved chef James Hemings's contributions to the American culinary canon, including his macaroni pie, a dish we now call mac and cheese.

True to the layered macaroni pie of Hemings's day, our version layers cooked pasta with butter and cheese, rather than a béchamel sauce. We also add cubed Virginia ham, an ingredient famous in Hemings's day as well as our own. Our recipe does have a few modern twists: rich and tangy cream cheese to help emulsify the sauce and chopped scallions to add a bit of bite.

YIELD: 4 servings
PREP TIME: 20 minutes
COOK TIME: 45 minutes

4 tablespoons unsalted butter, plus more for greasing

2¼ cups milk, divided

12 ounces small pasta shells

3 scallions, thinly sliced

6 ounces Virginia ham, cut into ½-inch pieces

8 ounces sharp cheddar cheese, coarsely grated

2 ounces cream cheese

Kosher salt and freshly ground black pepper

Hot sauce for serving (optional)

1 Preheat the oven to 350°F/177°C with a rack in the center position. Lightly butter an 8-inch square baking dish. Cut the 4 tablespoons of butter into small pieces.

2 In a large saucepan, bring 2 quarts of salted water to a boil. Add 2 cups of the milk and the pasta. Cook the pasta according to package directions until it is al dente. Drain the pasta into a colander.

3 Transfer a third of the pasta to the prepared baking dish. Top with a third of the scallions, ham, grated cheese, and butter. Dot with half of the cream cheese. Season with a pinch each of salt and pepper. Repeat with another third of the pasta, scallions, ham, grated cheese, and butter. Dot with the remaining half of the cream cheese. Season with salt and pepper. Top with the remaining pasta, scallions, ham, grated cheese, and butter. Pour the remaining ¼ cup of milk over the top.

4 Cover the baking dish with aluminum foil. Transfer to the oven. Bake for 25 to 30 minutes, until the cheeses are melted and the macaroni and cheese is bubbling around the edges.

5 Remove from the oven. Let stand for 5 minutes, then uncover and gently stir to combine. Serve with a few dashes of hot sauce, if desired.

QUEST FOR AN IRON LEGEND

Medieval Mushroom Orecchiette with Parmigiano & Parsley

On *Iron Chef: Quest for an Iron Legend*, chefs Gabriela Cámara, Dominique Crenn, Curtis Stone, and Marcus Samuelsson create a magical and medieval-inspired feast using three ingredients, each announced at a different time during the competition. One of the ingredients, mushrooms, has a unique connection with host chef Kristen Kish.

In another cooking competition, Chef Kish roasted mushrooms to reduce their moisture before sautéing them for a judge-pleasing side dish. In our take on the recipe, we follow Chef Kish's lead by roasting a mix of cremini and porcini mushrooms before cooking them into a velvety sauce tossed with orecchiette.

YIELD: 4 servings
PREP TIME: 15 minutes
COOK TIME: 1 hour

🌱 VEGETARIAN

1 pound cremini mushrooms, cleaned and quartered

4 ounces porcini mushrooms, cleaned and quartered

2 tablespoons olive oil

Kosher salt and freshly ground black pepper

4 tablespoons butter, divided

1 shallot, finely chopped

2 garlic cloves, finely chopped

2 tablespoons sherry vinegar

¼ cup low-sodium vegetable stock

¾ cup heavy cream

1 pound orecchiette pasta

1 small bunch fresh parsley (about ½ ounce), coarsely chopped

½ ounce Parmigiano Reggiano, finely grated

WATCH
IRON CHEF: QUEST FOR AN IRON LEGEND

1 Preheat the oven to 425°F/218°C with an oven rack in the center position. Place the mushrooms on a rimmed baking sheet. Toss with the olive oil, then season with salt and pepper.

2 Transfer the mushrooms to the oven, then roast for about 25 minutes, until the mushrooms are browned and tender. Meanwhile, bring a large pot of salted water to a boil.

3 In a large skillet, melt 2 tablespoons of the butter over medium heat. Add the shallot and garlic to the skillet, then cook for 2 to 3 minutes, until softened. Increase the heat to medium-high, then add the mushrooms to the same skillet. Stir the mushrooms with the shallot and garlic, then cook, without stirring, for 3 to 4 minutes, until the mushrooms are fragrant and beginning to brown.

4 Add the vinegar to the skillet with the mushrooms. Cook, stirring, for about 1 minute, until the liquid has nearly evaporated. Add the chicken stock and heavy cream to the skillet and bring to a simmer, then reduce the heat to medium-low. Cook, stirring occasionally, for 5 to 7 minutes, until the sauce has reduced slightly and is thick enough to coat the back of a spoon.

5 Add the orecchiette to the pot of boiling water, then cook according to package directions until it is al dente. Reserve ½ cup of the pasta cooking water, then drain the pasta. Return the pasta to the large pot.

6 Add the mushroom sauce, the remaining 2 tablespoons of butter, ¼ cup of the pasta water, and half of each the parsley and Parmigiano to the pot with the pasta. Over low heat, cook, stirring, until the butter and Parmigiano have melted into the sauce and the sauce coats the pasta, about 1 minute. Add the remaining ¼ cup of pasta water, 1 tablespoon at a time, if the sauce seems too thick.

7 Transfer the pasta and sauce to four shallow pasta bowls, then garnish with the remaining parsley and Parmigiano.

Southern-Style Pulled Chicken Banh Mi with Pickled Veggie Slaw & Grilled Bologna

During the "Tournament of Sandwiches" episode of *The American Barbecue Showdown*, contestant Tina consistently impresses judges Kevin Bludso and Melissa Cookston with her global flavors. In the first of the three challenges, Tina makes a Southern banh mi with pickle-brined smoked chicken, pickled veggies, and fried bologna in place of the usual paté.

For our streamlined version, we grill the chicken thighs and add a little smoked paprika both to the brine and as a pre-grilling rub. A crisp slaw with pickled veggies, crunchy fried shallots, plenty of fresh cilantro, and grilled bologna complete the sandwich. As both of the judges were mayo fans, feel free to add more if you like!

YIELD: 4 servings
PREP TIME: 30 minutes, plus 4 hours brining
COOK TIME: 30 minutes

PULLED CHICKEN

2 jalapeños, divided

2 pounds boneless, skinless chicken thighs

2 garlic cloves, peeled and crushed

½-inch piece fresh ginger, thinly sliced

1 cup dill pickle brine

2 teaspoons smoked paprika, divided

Freshly ground black pepper

Vegetable oil for cooking

Kosher salt

CRUNCHY SLAW

1 tablespoon granulated sugar

¾ teaspoon kosher salt

2 tablespoons rice vinegar

1 medium carrot, peeled and coarsely grated

4 radishes, trimmed and coarsely grated

3 scallions, trimmed and thinly sliced

½ small head Napa or green cabbage (about 8 ounces)

2 tablespoons vegetable oil

1 teaspoon toasted sesame oil

Freshly ground black pepper

12 slices bologna

2 baguettes

½ cup mayonnaise

⅓ cup store-bought fried shallots or onions

1 small bunch fresh cilantro (about ½ ounce)

Sriracha sauce for serving

>>recipe continues
on the next page

"I'm a big ol' bad barbecue sandwich."

—MELISSA COOKSTON

>>Southern-Style Pulled Chicken Banh Mi continued

1 **To brine the chicken:** Halve one of the jalapeños, then remove the stem and seeds (save the second jalapeño for step 7). Pat the chicken thighs dry. In a large resealable plastic bag, combine the garlic, ginger, halved jalapeño, chicken thighs, pickle brine, 1 teaspoon of smoked paprika, and a few grinds of pepper. Seal the bag, pressing out as much of the air as possible. Refrigerate the chicken in the brine for 4 hours. (If you are ever a contestant on *The American Barbecue Showdown*, you will have to settle for less brining time.)

2 **To make the slaw:** In a medium bowl, combine the sugar, salt, and vinegar, whisking until the sugar and salt dissolve. Add the carrot and radishes to the same bowl, then gently squeeze the mixture a few times with your hands to combine. Let stand at room temperature for 5 minutes. (The pickled vegetables can now be refrigerated for up to a week before you finish the slaw.)

3 Thinly slice 2 cups of cabbage (save any remaining cabbage for your own use). Add the scallions, sliced cabbage, vegetable oil, and sesame oil to the bowl with the pickled carrot and radishes. Stir to combine, then season to taste with salt and pepper.

4 **To grill the chicken:** Remove the chicken from the brine. Discard the brine and pat the chicken dry. Drizzle the chicken with vegetable oil, then season all over with salt, pepper, and the remaining 1 teaspoon of smoked paprika.

5 Lightly oil a grill or grill pan, then place over medium-high heat. Transfer the chicken thighs to the grill, then cook, turning occasionally, for 10 to 12 minutes, until the chicken is lightly charred and cooked through. Remove the chicken to a bowl, then let it rest for 5 to 10 minutes. (Keep the grill on for step 6.)

6 Brush the bologna slices with oil, then transfer to the grill. Cook for 1 to 2 minutes per side, until the bologna is warm and lightly charred, then transfer to a plate.

7 Shred the chicken with forks into bite-sized pieces. Remove the stem and seeds from the remaining jalapeño, then thinly slice it. Trim the ends from the baguettes, then cut each baguette into two 6-inch sections. Cut each piece in half lengthwise.

8 **To assemble the sandwiches:** Spread the cut sides of the baguettes with mayonnaise, then top four of the halves with the grilled bologna, pulled chicken, slaw, fried shallots or onions, and cilantro sprigs. Top with sliced jalapeños and as much or as little sriracha sauce as you like. Top with the remaining baguette halves.

CHEF'S TABLE

Cacio e Pepe

On May 20, 2012, an earthquake shook Italy, with the epicenter near the city of Modena. During the earthquake and the aftershocks, 360,000 large wheels of Parmigiano Reggiano were damaged, threatening the cheese makers' livelihood. In his episode of *Chef's Table*, Chef Massimo Bottura describes a solution he proposed to the Parmigiano consortium: a risotto inspired by the famous cacio e pepe, but using Parmigiano in place of the traditional Pecorino cheese. A global dinner was planned where people all over the world would make the recipe and the damaged Parmigiano could be used. In the end, 40,000 people made the recipe and the Parmigiano makers were saved.

Cacio e pepe is a classic Italian recipe and many versions of the recipe exist, but all use the same three core ingredients: Pecorino cheese, pasta, and black peppercorns. Inspired by Chef Bottura, our recipe uses Parmigiano instead of Pecorino cheese.

YIELD: 4 servings **PREP TIME:** 15 minutes **COOK TIME:** 15 minutes  **VEGETARIAN**

2 tablespoons whole black peppercorns, plus more for serving

Kosher salt

12 ounces spaghetti alla chitarra or spaghetti

6 ounces Parmigiano Reggiano, finely grated

1 Place a small skillet over medium heat. Add 2 tablespoons of peppercorns to the skillet, then toast, shaking the skillet occasionally, for 1 to 2 minutes, until the peppercorns are aromatic. Transfer to a small bowl. Pulse the peppercorns in a spice mill or crush in a mortar and pestle until finely ground. (Alternatively, transfer to a pepper mill and grind.)

2 Bring a large pot of salted water to a boil. Cook the pasta according to package directions until it is al dente. Reserve ½ cup of the pasta water. Drain the pasta, then immediately return it to the pot. Add half of the peppercorns and several large pinches of the Parmigiano, then start stirring quickly with tongs or a fork. Add the remaining Parmigiano in large pinches, stirring constantly. Loosen with the reserved pasta water, 1 tablespoon at a time, until the cheese has melted and the pasta is coated in a smooth sauce. Season the pasta to taste with salt and more pepper, then serve.

WATCH CHEF'S TABLE

IS IT CAKE?

Hamburger Cake

On *Is It Cake?* contestants pull out all the stops—and the fondant and the special baking equipment—to make delicious pastry creations that perfectly mimic different objects, all in the hopes of fooling the judges.

Our version may not fool anyone at your favorite local burger place, but with a rich yellow cake bun that is "toasted" with salted caramel buttercream, crispy and chocolatey "burger" patties, cream cheese condiments, and more, it is sure to be the star of your next gathering.

YIELD: One 9-inch cake
PREP TIME: 30 minutes
COOK TIME: 2 hours 30 minutes, plus chilling

 VEGETARIAN

"BUN" CAKE

Nonstick baking spray

1¼ cups all-purpose flour

1 teaspoon baking powder

½ teaspoon baking soda

½ teaspoon ground turmeric

½ teaspoon kosher salt

1 small orange

4 tablespoons unsalted butter

1 large egg

¾ cup granulated sugar

1 cup buttermilk

¼ cup vegetable oil

1 teaspoon pure vanilla extract

"BURGER PATTIES"

½ cup unsalted butter

½ cup unsweetened Dutch process cocoa powder

¾ teaspoon kosher salt

One 14-ounce can sweetened condensed milk

20 soft caramels, unwrapped

One 10-ounce bag mini marshmallows

5 cups chocolate puffed rice cereal

"LETTUCE"

2½ cups unsweetened coconut flakes

Green food coloring

Yellow food coloring

"BUN" FROSTING

½ cup unsalted butter, softened

1½ cups confectioners' sugar

¼ cup salted caramel sauce, plus more if desired, at room temperature

¼ teaspoon pure vanilla extract

¼ teaspoon kosher salt

Poppy seeds, toasted sesame seeds, or puffed rice cereal for garnishing

"KETCHUP, MAYO & MUSTARD"

One 8-ounce package cream cheese, softened

½ cup sour cream

½ cup confectioners' sugar

1 teaspoon pure vanilla extract

½ teaspoon kosher salt

Yellow food coloring

Red food coloring

>>recipe continues on the next page

>>Hamburger Cake continued

1 **To make the bun cake:** Preheat the oven to 350°F/177°C with a rack in the center position. Lightly coat an 8-inch round cake pan with nonstick spray, then line the bottom with parchment paper.

2 To a medium bowl, add the flour, baking powder, baking soda, turmeric, and salt. Whisk to combine. Finely grate the zest of the orange. In a small saucepan, combine the butter and orange zest, then heat over low for 3 to 4 minutes, until the butter melts. (Alternatively, the butter and zest can be melted in the microwave.)

3 In a large bowl, whisk the egg and sugar until combined, then add the melted butter, buttermilk, oil, and vanilla and whisk until smooth. Sprinkle the dry ingredients over the wet, then stir until just combined. Scrape the cake batter into the prepared baking pan, then smooth the top with a spatula.

4 Transfer the bun cake to the oven. Bake for about 35 minutes, until the cake is golden brown and springs back lightly to the touch. Remove from the oven and transfer to a wire cooling rack. Let the cake cool for 10 minutes. Carefully invert the cake onto a cooling rack, then flip it back right side up on another. Cool completely.

5 **To make the burger patties:** Line two baking sheets with parchment paper, tracing a 9-inch circle on each piece of paper. Lightly coat the baking sheet with nonstick spray, then set aside.

6 In a large saucepan, combine the butter and cocoa powder. Warm over low heat, whisking frequently, for 3 to 4 minutes, until the butter is melted. Add the salt and condensed milk, then stir to combine. Next, add all of the caramels, then continue stirring until all are melted. (The mixture may look broken and this is okay.)

7 Add the marshmallows to the same saucepan, then turn off the heat. Stir until just melted, then, working quickly, stir in the chocolate puffed rice cereal.

8 Scrape half of the mixture into the circle outline on each sheet of parchment paper. Use a spatula to pat the chocolate mixture into a 9-inch round with an even thickness. Let set at room temperature for about 45 minutes, until firm.

9 **To make the lettuce:** In a large resealable plastic bag, combine the coconut flakes, 6 drops of green food coloring, 3 drops of yellow food coloring, and 1 teaspoon of water. Seal the bag, then shake it to combine the colors and coat the coconut, adding another drop or two of food coloring as needed. Spread the "lettuce" out on a plate to dry.

10 **To make the bun frosting:** In a medium bowl, use a hand mixer to beat the butter on medium speed for about 5 minutes, scraping down the bowl as needed, until light and fluffy. Add half of the confectioners' sugar, then beat on low until fully incorporated. Repeat with the remaining confectioners' sugar. Increase the mixer speed to medium-high and beat for about 3 minutes, until the mixture is very light and fluffy. Add ¼ cup of the caramel sauce, vanilla, and salt to the same bowl, beating on medium speed until just combined. Taste the frosting, adding another tablespoon or two of caramel sauce or an extra ½ teaspoon of salt, if desired. Transfer the bun frosting to a medium bowl. Clean the mixing bowl and beaters and reserve for step 11.

11 **To make the ketchup, mayo, and mustard frostings:** Add the cream cheese to the reserved bowl. Using the hand mixer, beat on medium speed for 3 to 4 minutes, until light and fluffy. Add the sour cream, then beat on medium speed for 2 to 3 minutes, until incorporated, scraping down the bowl as needed. Add half of the confectioners' sugar, then beat on low speed for 1 to 2 minutes, until incorporated. Add the remaining confectioners' sugar, vanilla, and salt. Beat on low speed until the sugar is incorporated, 1 to 2 minutes. Increase to medium-high and beat for 2 to 3 minutes, until very light and fluffy.

12 Divide the cream cheese frosting into three bowls. To the first bowl, add yellow food coloring, a drop or two at a time to make the "mustard." To the second bowl, add a few drops of red and one drop of yellow to reach the orange red of ketchup, adding more red and yellow food coloring, a drop or two at a time, as needed. Leave the third bowl plain for the "mayonnaise."

13 **To assemble:** Using a serrated knife, split the burger cake into two layers. Spread a thin layer of the salted caramel buttercream on the domed "top bun" and around the sides of the second "bottom bun" layer. Transfer to the refrigerator and chill for 15 minutes, until the crumb layer is set.

14 Spread the remaining salted caramel buttercream around the sides of the bottom layer and on the sides and top of the domed layer. Sprinkle the top layer with poppy seeds, sesame seeds, or puffed rice cereal. Carefully transfer the bottom layer to a platter or cake stand.

15 Spread the plain cream cheese frosting over the bottom layer, swooping it with a spatula, and allowing some of it to hang over the edges. Top the cream cheese frosting with a third of the "lettuce." Top with one chocolate "burger patty." Spread the red cream cheese frosting over the patty, then top with another third of the "lettuce." Top the second chocolate "patty" with the yellow cream cheese frosting and the remaining "lettuce." Top with the domed cake layer. Transfer to the refrigerator and chill for 15 minutes before serving.

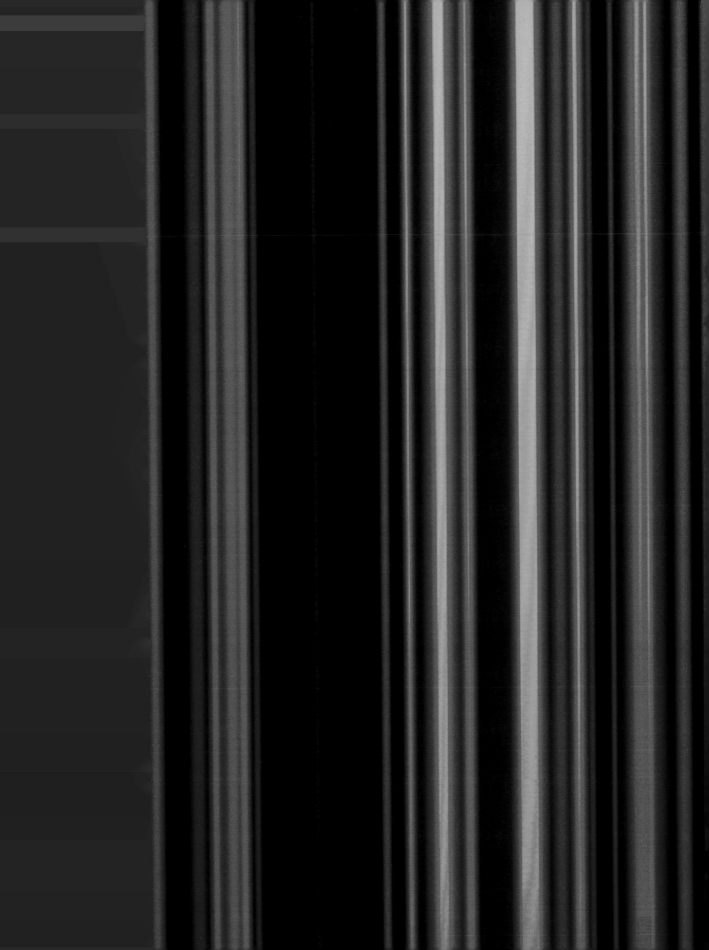

All in the Family Food

Gather your near and dear
together for a meal in front
of these family-centric shows.

ALL IN THE FAMILY FOOD

Peach Cornbread

In the very first episode of *Family Reunion*, Ami McKellan hides a pan of M'Dear's cornbread under the table when Uncle Daniel breezes through. Uncle Daniel may pack up much of the food on the table for a date later that evening, but there is still a whole pan of cornbread and a full bowl of M'Dear's delicious banana pudding left to enjoy.

Southern cornbread (probably M'Dear's, too) is usually unsweetened. Borrowing inspiration from Georgia's famous peaches and the show's Columbus, Georgia, setting, we make a lightly sweet skillet version with chunks of juicy peaches folded in. We finish our peach cornbread with lots of hot honey butter. This delicious, if unconventional, cornbread might just be a hit at M'Dear's, and maybe at your next family reunion, as well.

YIELD: One 8-inch skillet   **PREP TIME:** 10 minutes   **COOK TIME:** 40 minutes    **VEGETARIAN**

11 tablespoons unsalted butter, divided

2 large peaches (10 to 12 ounces)

1 cup plus 1 tablespoon all-purpose flour, divided

1 cup cornmeal, preferably stone-ground

2 teaspoons baking powder

1 teaspoon kosher salt

2 large eggs

1¼ cups buttermilk

5 tablespoons honey, divided

Pinch of crushed red pepper flakes

Kosher salt and freshly ground black pepper

1 Place an 8-inch cast-iron skillet on the center rack of the oven, then preheat the oven to 425°F/218°C. Put 5 tablespoons of the butter on the counter to soften. Add the remaining 6 tablespoons of butter to a small microwave-safe bowl. Microwave on high in 30-second increments until melted.

2 Peel the peaches, if desired, then cut them into ½-inch pieces. Place them in a medium bowl and toss with 1 tablespoon of the flour.

3 In a large bowl, combine the cornmeal, baking powder, salt, and the remaining 1 cup of flour, whisking until incorporated. Crack the eggs into a second medium bowl, then whisk until the yolks and whites are fully combined. Add the buttermilk, 3 tablespoons of the honey, and the melted butter to the bowl with the eggs, then whisk to combine. Pour the wet ingredients into the dry, then stir until just combined. Fold in the peaches.

4 Carefully remove the hot cast-iron skillet from the oven. Add 1 table-spoon of the softened butter to the skillet, then brush the butter onto the bottom and sides of the skillet. Pour in the cornbread batter, then smooth the top with a spatula.

5 Transfer the cornbread to the oven, then reduce the oven temperature to 400°F/204°C. Bake for 25 to 30 minutes, until the cornbread is lightly browned on top and a toothpick inserted into the center comes out clean. Remove from the oven and cool slightly.

6 While the cornbread bakes, in a small bowl, combine the remaining 4 tablespoons of softened butter, the remaining 2 tablespoons of honey, a pinch or two of crushed red pepper flakes (more or less depending on your heat preference), a pinch of salt, and a few grinds of pepper. Stir to combine, adding more salt, pepper, or crushed red pepper flakes to taste. Cut the cornbread into wedges and serve the hot honey butter alongside.

ROMA

Turkey Tortas

In the Academy Award-winning movie *Roma*, Cleo and her friend meet their boyfriends and have a torta at La Casa del Pavo. While *Roma* is set in the early 1970s, the restaurant is still open today, serving a menu that includes the braised turkey tortas that Cleo and her friend might have shared.

Many turkey torta recipes use roasted turkey, but the tortas at La Casa del Pavo used spiced, braised turkey. In our *Roma*-inspired torta, we braise bone-in, skin-on turkey thighs with spices, citrus, and chiles de árbol until tender and very flavorful. (You could also use the same weight of turkey legs.) The meat is cooled, shredded, and then piled on soft telera rolls with sliced avocado, chopped onions, cilantro, salsa verde, and pickled jalapeños.

YIELD: 4 tortas
PREP TIME: 30 minutes
COOK TIME: 3 hours

BRAISED TURKEY

4 bone-in, skin-on turkey thighs (about 5 pounds)

1 tablespoon kosher salt, divided

2 teaspoons smoked paprika

1 teaspoon ground cumin

½ teaspoon freshly ground black pepper

1 tablespoon vegetable oil

1 yellow onion, halved and thinly sliced

4 garlic cloves, peeled and crushed

1 medium orange, thinly sliced

2 limes, one thinly sliced and one left whole

1 chipotle pepper in adobo sauce, finely chopped

4 bay leaves

1 tablespoon dried oregano

2 teaspoons paprika

2 whole cinnamon sticks

2 dried chiles de árbol

6 cups low-sodium chicken broth

TORTAS

4 telera rolls, split

2 ripe avocados, halved, pitted, and thinly sliced

1 small white onion, finely chopped

1 small bunch fresh cilantro (about ½ ounce), finely chopped

Salsa verde for serving

Pickled jalapeños and carrots for serving

1 **To braise the turkey:** Pat the turkey thighs dry. In a small bowl, combine 2 teaspoons of the salt, smoked paprika, cumin, and pepper. Season the turkey thighs all over with the spice mixture, patting gently to help the seasoning adhere.

2 In a large Dutch oven, heat the vegetable oil over medium-high. Transfer the turkey thighs to the pot, skin side down. Cook, shifting the pot as needed to ensure even browning, for 10 to 12 minutes, until the skin is deeply browned.

3 Once the turkey skin has browned, flip over the thighs and add the onion and garlic to the pot. Continue cooking over medium-high heat, scraping the browned bits off the bottom with a wooden spoon, for 3 to 4 minutes, until the onion has softened and the garlic is fragrant.

4 To the same pot, add the orange and lime slices, chipotle pepper in adobo sauce, bay leaves, oregano, paprika, cinnamon, chiles de árbol, and chicken broth. Bring to a boil, then partially cover and reduce to a simmer. Cook for 2 to 2½ hours, until the turkey meat is very tender.

5 Transfer the turkey thighs to a plate and let stand for about 10 minutes, until cool enough to handle. Strain the braising liquid through a fine-mesh strainer. Discard the solids and reserve the braising liquid for step 6.

6 Remove the turkey meat, then tear it into bite-sized pieces. (The skin and bones can either be discarded or saved for making stock.) Add the turkey meat to a bowl, then stir in ¼ cup of the braising liquid (see Fast Forward pro tip on using leftover braising liquid). Season the turkey to taste with salt and pepper, then cover to keep warm.

7 **To assemble the tortas:** Divide the braised turkey among the rolls, then squeeze the remaining whole lime over the top. Layer the avocados, onion, and cilantro on top of the turkey. Spoon a little salsa verde over the top and serve with pickled jalapeños and carrots, either on the tortas or on the side.

▶▶ **Fast forward**

Pro tip! After the turkey thighs have braised, you will be left with the rich, flavorful braising liquid. Cool the liquid then save as a base for your next batch of chicken tortilla soup or chili. Alternatively, season the liquid with salt to taste and then sip as a warming, nourishing bone broth.

OŻARK

Pancakes for Dinner

In their final dinner together in season three of *Ozark*, Wendy and her brother, Ben, order pancakes and bacon at a diner. After asking Ben about his hopes for the future, she abandons him at the restaurant, leaving him to his fate at Nelson's hands. You will definitely need a box of tissues for the episodes that follow, and you will also need a stack of these diner-style pancakes, too. The bacon is optional, but Ben would like it if you decided to have some.

Malt powder gives these plate-sized pancakes a uniquely diner flavor, but if you can't find it or prefer not to buy it, you can use 3 tablespoons of granulated sugar and an extra ½ teaspoon of vanilla extract instead.

YIELD: 4 servings   **PREP TIME:** 10 minutes   **COOK TIME:** 25 minutes

VEGETARIAN (without optional bacon)

2 cups all-purpose flour

¼ cup malt powder

2 teaspoons baking powder

1 teaspoon baking soda

1 teaspoon kosher salt

4 tablespoons unsalted butter, plus more for serving

2 large eggs

3 cups buttermilk

½ teaspoon pure vanilla extract

Vegetable oil for cooking

Maple or pancake syrup for serving

Crispy bacon for serving (optional)

1 To a medium bowl, add the flour, malt powder, baking powder, baking soda, and salt, then whisk until combined. Put 4 tablespoons of butter in a small microwave-safe dish, then heat on high in 30-second increments, until melted.

2 Crack the eggs into a large bowl, then whisk until fully combined. Add the buttermilk and vanilla, then whisk until no streaks of buttermilk remain. Sprinkle the dry ingredients over the buttermilk mixture, then stir with a rubber spatula until just combined. (There will be lumps in the batter.) Add the melted butter to the same bowl, then stir until no streaks of butter remain. Let the batter stand at room temperature for 15 minutes.

3 Preheat the oven to its lowest setting, usually between 180°F/82°C and 200°F/93°C, with a rack in the center position. Place a rimmed baking sheet next to the stove.

4 Brush a large two-burner griddle or large cast-iron skillet with vegetable oil, then place over medium heat. Transfer ½-cup portions of the batter, 2 inches apart, onto the hot griddle. After about 2 minutes, when bubbles appear on the surface of the pancakes and the edges are set, flip the pancakes and continue cooking, for about 1 minute more, until the second side is golden brown and the pancake is cooked through. Transfer the pancakes to the baking sheet, then keep warm in the oven. Repeat with the remaining batter, greasing the griddle or skillet between batches. Please note: The cooking time will shorten as the griddle gets hotter. If the pancakes are browning too quickly, reduce the heat to medium-low.

5 Serve the warm pancakes with syrup, more butter, and crispy bacon, if desired.

ON MY BLOCK

Ruby Red Pozole

2 pounds boneless pork shoulder

1 pound pork spareribs

Kosher salt and freshly ground black pepper

Vegetable oil for cooking

2 large white onions, divided

9 garlic cloves, divided

3 bay leaves

1½ teaspoons dried oregano

1 large bunch fresh cilantro (about 1 ounce), divided

1 small bunch fresh mint (about ¼ ounce)

6 dried guajillo chiles, stemmed and seeded

4 dried ancho chiles, stemmed and seeded

½ cup ice

One 29-ounce can hominy

¼ small head iceberg lettuce or green cabbage (about 4 ounces)

6 radishes, thinly sliced

2 limes, cut into wedges

1 ripe avocado, peeled, pitted, and cut into ½-inch pieces

2 cups tortilla strips or chips

On Netflix's teen comedy-drama *On My Block*, friends Monse, César, Ruby, and Jamal navigate challenges both large and small as they get ready to start high school. For Ruby, the joy of having his own room after his older brother leaves for college ends abruptly. No sooner has Ruby started to imagine the possibilities than his mother announces that his *abuelita* and her nearly life-size nativity figurines will be moving into the room as well. But her presence becomes more of a comfort as they grow closer.

A bowl of this hearty, deeply soothing pozole will keep you going through any teenage drama—whether you're actually living it or just watching it on TV. Pozole takes time to make, but like getting to the final episodes of *On My Block*'s four amazing seasons on Netflix, it's 100 percent worth the wait.

YIELD: 4 servings
PREP TIME: 1 hour
COOK TIME: 3 hours 45 minutes

 **GLUTEN FREE**

1 Pat the pork shoulder dry, then cut it into 2-inch pieces. Pat the spareribs dry, then season both the pork shoulder and spareribs all over with salt and pepper. In a large Dutch oven, heat 1 tablespoon of the vegetable oil over medium-high. Working in batches, add the pork shoulder and cook for 7 to 8 minutes, until browned all over. Repeat with the remaining pork shoulder and then with the spareribs, adding more oil as needed.

2 Peel one of the onions, then cut it into quarters. Peel the garlic cloves, then lightly crush them with a knife.

3 Return all of the browned pork to the Dutch oven along with the onion quarters, 6 of the garlic cloves, all of the bay leaves, oregano, half of the cilantro, and all of the mint. Add enough cold water to cover the pork by 1 inch. Cover and bring to a boil. Reduce the heat to a simmer, then cook, covered, for 2 to 2½ hours, until the pork is very tender and falling off the bone.

4 Meanwhile, place a medium skillet over medium heat. Add half of the guajillo and ancho chiles to the skillet, then cook, stirring occasionally, for 1 to 2 minutes, until toasted and fragrant. Place the chiles in a medium bowl, then repeat with the remaining chiles.

>>recipe continues on the next page

5 Cover the toasted chiles with boiling water, then let stand at room temperature for about 25 minutes, until softened. Peel and finely chop the second white onion.

6 Once the pork is tender, use a slotted spoon to transfer the pork shoulder and spareribs to a plate. Once the meat is cool enough to handle, tear the meat into bite-sized pieces, discarding any excess fat or bones.

7 Set a colander over a large heatproof bowl, then strain the cooking liquid and discard any solids. Add the ice to the broth, then let stand for 5 minutes. Skim off any fat or oil that rises to the top of the pork broth. Set the Dutch oven aside for step 9.

8 Using a slotted spoon, transfer the softened chiles to a blender or food processor, then discard the soaking liquid. Add ½ cup of the chopped onion, the remaining 3 garlic cloves, ⅔ cup of the defatted pork broth, and 1 teaspoon of salt. Blend until very smooth and about the thickness of applesauce, adding more broth, 1 tablespoon at a time, as needed. Set a fine-mesh sieve over a medium bowl. Pour the chili paste through the sieve, pressing on the solids to help the liquid come through. Discard any remaining solids.

9 In the reserved Dutch oven, heat 1 tablespoon of vegetable oil over medium-low heat. Add the chili paste, then cook, stirring occasionally, for 5 to 7 minutes, until fragrant and thickened slightly.

10 Drain the hominy. Add the hominy and 2 quarts of the pork broth to the same Dutch oven. Bring to a boil, then reduce the heat to medium. Cook, stirring occasionally, for about 20 minutes, until the broth has reduced slightly and the hominy is warm. Season the broth to taste with salt and pepper. Return the pork and any accumulated juices to the Dutch oven, then cook for 5 to 10 minutes, until the pork is warm.

11 While the pork is simmering, thinly slice the lettuce or cabbage. Ladle the pozole into four shallow bowls, then garnish at the table with the remaining chopped onion, sliced radishes, lime wedges, avocado, lettuce, and tortilla strips or chips.

YES DAY
Gut-Buster Parfait

In the movie *Yes Day*, the Torres family accepts a local ice cream parlor's challenge to eat a whole, gigantic sundae in just 30 minutes. Even when the kids start to fill up, Allison and Carlos's parents who always say no, say yes to the sundae and manage to finish the last bites.

For our take on the Gut-Buster sundae, we make a wonderful, wacky hybrid dessert, something between a trifle and a sundae, layering scoops of ice cream with a confetti whipped cream, crushed cookies, candy, and more. How many does this serve? Well, likely eight or more on a normal day, but on your own Yes Day? Probably four.

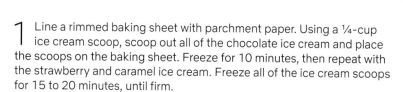

YIELD: 8 servings
PREP TIME: 25 minutes, plus chilling
COOK TIME: 20 minutes

 VEGETARIAN CONTAINS NUTS

1 pint chocolate ice cream

1 pint strawberry ice cream

1 pint caramel ice cream

12 peanut butter sandwich cookies

12 chocolate sandwich cookies

12 shortbread cookies

1 pint heavy cream

⅓ cup sour cream

¾ cup rainbow sprinkles, divided

1 cup honey roasted peanuts

1 cup chocolate coated candies

1 cup mini marshmallows

1 cup hot fudge sauce

1 cup salted caramel sauce

Maraschino cherries for garnishing

1 Line a rimmed baking sheet with parchment paper. Using a ¼-cup ice cream scoop, scoop out all of the chocolate ice cream and place the scoops on the baking sheet. Freeze for 10 minutes, then repeat with the strawberry and caramel ice cream. Freeze all of the ice cream scoops for 15 to 20 minutes, until firm.

2 Reserve three of each type of cookie for garnishing. Place the remaining cookies in a large resealable plastic bag. Seal the bag, then use a rolling pin to coarsely crush the cookies.

3 In a large bowl (or in a mixer bowl fitted with the whisk attachment), beat the heavy cream on medium speed for about 5 minutes, until soft peaks form. Add the sour cream, then whip until stiff peaks form. Fold in ½ cup of the rainbow sprinkles.

4 In a 3-quart trifle bowl or large serving bowl, make a cookie layer with one-third of the crushed cookies, then top with one-third of the ice cream scoops. Top the ice cream with ¼ cup each of peanuts, chocolate coated candies, and mini marshmallows. Drizzle with ¼ cup of hot fudge sauce and salted caramel sauce, then spoon 1 cup of the whipped cream over the top. Repeat to make two more layers of cookie crumbs, ice cream, peanuts, chocolate coated candies, marshmallows, hot fudge sauce, caramel sauce, and whipped cream.

5 Decorate the top of the sundae with the reserved whole cookies, remaining peanuts, chocolate coated candies, mini marshmallows, hot fudge sauce, and caramel sauce. Garnish with the remaining ¼ cup of sprinkles and as many maraschino cherries as you like. Eat immediately, either *Yes Day* style out of the serving bowl, or scooped into individual servings.

Flavors from Around the World

Netflix is available for streaming in more than 190 countries, a handful of which can be found in this smorgasbord of recipes.

MONEY HEIST

(LA CASA DE PAPEL)

Melon & Royal Mint of Spain Salad

Full of classic Spanish ingredients—jamón ibérico, sherry vinegar, and Marcona almonds—this salad is a beautiful balance of sweet and savory, crispy and juicy. The dish is also a perfect accompaniment for the edge-of-your-seat thriller *Money Heist (La Casa de Papel),* in which the first season finds eight accomplished thieves planning an elaborate robbery of the Royal Mint of Spain. And the series gets even more insane and memorable—proving that great stories can come from anywhere and entertain audiences around the world. *Money Heist (La Casa de Papel)* continues to be one of Netflix's most popular international titles of all time.

Fresh figs are delicious in this dish, but if you can't find them, chunks of ripe tomato would make a tasty substitute.

YIELD: 4 servings   **PREP TIME:** 10 minutes   **COOK TIME:** 5 minutes    **GLUTEN FREE**

2 tablespoons plus 2 teaspoons extra virgin olive oil, divided

2 ounces jamón ibérico or prosciutto

1½ teaspoons sherry vinegar

Kosher salt and freshly ground black pepper

Half of a small cantaloupe (about 1½ pounds)

1 pint fresh figs

1 small bunch fresh mint (about ½ ounce) for garnishing

2 ounces Marcona almonds or roasted salted almonds, coarsely chopped

1 In a medium nonstick skillet, heat 2 teaspoons of the olive oil over medium. Add the jamón ibérico or prosciutto to the skillet in an even layer. Cook, turning occasionally, for about 3 minutes, until browned in spots and beginning to crisp. Transfer to a paper towel–lined plate to cool. Tear the cooled ham into large pieces.

2 Add the vinegar to a medium bowl. Whisk in the remaining 2 tablespoons of olive oil in a slow, steady stream, then season to taste with salt and pepper.

3 Using a sharp knife, carefully remove the cantaloupe rind, then scoop out the seeds. Cut the cantaloupe into 1-inch chunks. Cut off the fig stems, then halve figs lengthwise (quarter them if large). Remove the mint leaves from the stems and tear them into bite-sized pieces.

4 On a serving platter, arrange the cantaloupe chunks and figs, then spoon the sherry vinaigrette over the top. Scatter the crispy ham and almonds over the top as well. Garnish with the mint. Season with salt and pepper and drizzle with a little extra olive oil.

Extraordinary Attorney Woo

Haengbok Noodles

PORK BROTH

1 pound pork bones

1¼ cups mirin, divided

1 large white onion, peeled and cut into quarters

6 garlic cloves, peeled

4 bay leaves

7 black peppercorns

PORK BELLY

1 pound pork belly

2 scallions, trimmed

3 garlic cloves, peeled and crushed

2 teaspoons kosher salt, plus more for seasoning

Freshly ground black pepper

CHILI PASTE

2 garlic cloves, finely chopped

1 tablespoon gochugaru, plus more for garnishing

1½ teaspoons gochujang

1 tablespoon mirin

1 teaspoon soy sauce

Freshly ground black pepper

6 scallions

2 medium carrots

8 ounces thin wheat noodles, such as Korean somyeon noodles

During the episode "The Blue Night of Jeju II" of the South Korean show *Extraordinary Attorney Woo*, lead attorney Jung falls ill during a court appearance and is diagnosed with stomach cancer. He tells his team that the only food he wants to eat is the meat noodles from Haengbok Noodles. Finding the business shuttered under mysterious circumstances, Young-woo and her fellow attorneys search for the owner. After several dead ends, they find the owner cooking at a local temple and come up with a plan to help him get his restaurant back. Grateful, the owner makes the team noodles, which are every bit as good as Attorney Jung remembers.

More than just a plot point, Jeju meat noodles (a South Korean dish made with pork), are a real, delicious, and much sought-after dish. Like the search for the Haengbok Noodles, the beginning of this recipe does take some time, but it is very much worth the journey. First, pork bones are simmered with aromatics for 8 hours, a process that we make more hands-off by using a slow cooker. The broth can be made several days in advance or frozen for up to a month. Once the broth is ready, pork belly is simmered in the broth until tender. The sliced pork belly is served over chewy wheat noodles with ladlefuls of the soothing pork broth. A quick chili paste, grated carrots, and sliced scallions complete the dish.

YIELD: 4 servings   **PREP TIME:** 30 minutes
COOK TIME: 9 hours 30 minutes

1 **To make the pork broth:** In a large pot, combine the pork bones and ¼ cup of the mirin. Cover the bones with 2 inches of cold water. Bring to a boil over high heat, then cook for 5 minutes. Drain the bones and rinse with cold water.

2 Place the onion and pork bones in a slow cooker, then add the garlic, bay leaves, peppercorns, and the remaining 1 cup of mirin. Cover with 3 quarts of cold water. Cook the broth on low for 8 hours.

3 Place a colander over a large pot. Carefully strain the stock into the pot, then discard the bones, onion, garlic, bay leaves, and peppercorns.

4 **To cook the pork belly:** Place the pot with the pork broth on the stove top. Cover and bring to a boil over high heat. Carefully add the pork belly to the broth. Boil for 10 minutes, then reduce the heat to medium, cover, and simmer the meat for 20 minutes.

>>recipe continues on the next page

>>Haengbok Noodles continued

5 After the pork belly has simmered for 20 minutes, add the scallions, garlic, 2 teaspoons of kosher salt, and a few grinds of fresh pepper. Cover the pot and cook over medium heat for 20 to 30 minutes, until the pork belly is tender. Transfer the pork belly to a cutting board, then let rest for 5 to 10 minutes, until cool enough to slice. Discard the scallions and garlic. Season the broth to taste with salt and pepper.

6 **To make the chili paste:** In a small bowl, combine the garlic, 1 tablespoon of the gochugaru, gochujang, mirin, soy sauce, and 1 tablespoon of the pork broth. Stir to combine, then season with a few grinds of pepper.

7 **To prepare the garnishes and cook the noodles:** Thinly slice the scallions. Trim and peel the carrots, then either cut them into thin strips or grate them on the large holes of a box grater. Bring a medium pot of salted water to a boil. Add the noodles to the water, then cook, usually for about 3 minutes, until chewy and tender. Drain the noodles and rinse with cold water to stop the cooking.

8 Thinly slice the pork belly. Divide the noodles among four bowls. Arrange the pork belly over the top, then ladle some of the broth over both the pork and noodles. Garnish the pork and noodles with the scallions, carrots, and a pinch of gochugaru. Serve with the chili paste alongside, adding to the noodles to taste.

EMILY IN PARIS
Gabriel's Coq au Vin

Emily in Paris is a show that focuses on how one woman juggles work, friends, and romance. But it is also about delicious French food. Emily visits Camille's family's château and meets Gérard, Camille's father, who is lying naked by the pool. Gérard asks Emily if she has tasted Gabriel's *coq au vin*, telling her, "When it hit my lips, I was ready to propose to him!" *Coq au vin*, literally "rooster with wine," originated as a way to make an old bird tender, but nowadays this classic dish is most often made with a cut-up young whole chicken. This simplified version uses bone-in chicken thighs to keep things easy. Serve it with mashed or roasted potatoes, and maybe someone will want to propose to you, too.

YIELD: 6 servings   **PREP TIME:** 25 minutes   **COOK TIME:** 1 hour 40 minutes

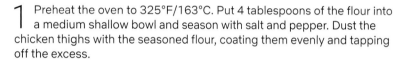

5 tablespoons all-purpose flour, divided

Fine sea salt and freshly ground black pepper

5 pounds bone-in, skinless chicken thighs

2 tablespoons unsalted butter, at room temperature, divided

10 shallots, roughly chopped

¼ pound thick-cut bacon slices, cut into ½-inch pieces

One 750-ml bottle dry red wine

9 ounces button mushrooms, cleaned and sliced

2 fresh thyme sprigs

1 bay leaf

Chopped fresh flat-leaf parsley for garnishing

1 Preheat the oven to 325°F/163°C. Put 4 tablespoons of the flour into a medium shallow bowl and season with salt and pepper. Dust the chicken thighs with the seasoned flour, coating them evenly and tapping off the excess.

2 In a large Dutch oven or other heavy ovenproof pot, melt 1 tablespoon of the butter over medium heat. Add the shallots and cook, stirring, for about 3 minutes, until beginning to soften. Add the bacon and continue to cook, stirring, for about 5 minutes, until the shallots are caramelized and the bacon is crisp. Using a slotted spoon, transfer the shallots and bacon to a plate.

3 Raise the heat to medium-high. Working in batches to avoid crowding, add the chicken thighs to the fat remaining in the pot and cook, turning once, for 5 to 8 minutes on each side, until the chicken is golden brown on both sides. As each batch is ready, transfer it to a plate. When all the chicken is browned, return the shallots and bacon to the pot. Pour in the wine, bring to a simmer, and deglaze the pot, scraping the pot bottom with a wooden spoon to dislodge any browned bits. Add the chicken pieces, mushrooms, thyme, and bay leaf, return to a simmer, and cook for 10 minutes. Cover the pot, transfer it to the oven, and cook for about 1 hour, until the chicken is so tender it is nearly falling off the bone.

4 Remove the pot from the oven and, using a slotted spoon, transfer the chicken to a plate. Cover the chicken with aluminum foil to keep it warm. Remove and discard the thyme sprigs and bay leaf.

5 In a small bowl, using a fork, work together the remaining 1 tablespoon each of flour and butter to form a uniform paste. Place the pot on the stove top and bring the contents to a boil over medium heat. Gradually whisk in the butter mixture until completely dissolved. Adjust the heat to maintain a simmer and simmer for about 15 minutes, until the liquid thickens.

6 Return the chicken to the pot and rewarm in the sauce for a few minutes, then serve, garnished with parsley.

Gabriel's Coq au Vin recipe, courtesy of *Emily in Paris: The Official Cookbook*, Weldon Owen (2022).

LITTLE THINGS

Onion Bhaji

When a bhaji craving strikes in the India-based series *Little Things*, Dhruv lures the reluctant Kavya out of bed and they head out in search of a specific roadside stand. Although the stand is closed, the pair find a winery for a tasting and a scenic spot to talk about the future.

Crispy, tempting bhaji are the perfect snack to sustain you through the ups and downs of Dhruv and Kavya's relationship in this rom-com set in Mumbai. Make sure to serve the spicy fritters with plenty of coriander chutney for dipping.

YIELD: 4 appetizer servings
PREP TIME: 10 minutes
COOK TIME: 20 minutes

 VEGAN   **GLUTEN FREE**

1 large yellow onion

1 teaspoon kosher salt, plus more for seasoning

1 small green chile, stemmed, seeded, and finely chopped

¼ teaspoon turmeric

½ teaspoon ground cumin

¼ teaspoon ground coriander

½ cup gram or chickpea flour

¼ cup rice flour

½ cup cold water

Vegetable oil for frying

Coriander chutney for serving

1 Halve the onion, then very thinly slice it crosswise (use a mandoline for the best results). In a medium bowl, combine the onion with 1 teaspoon of salt, then gently toss and squeeze with your hands to help the salt draw moisture out of the onion. Let stand for 5 minutes.

2 Add the chile to the bowl with the onion along with the turmeric, cumin, coriander, gram or chickpea flour, rice flour, and cold water. Combine with your hands or a spatula, until the seasonings are evenly mixed with the onion and the flours have formed a damp, slightly sticky batter.

3 In a medium pot, heat 2 inches of vegetable oil to 350°F/177°C. Line a plate with paper towels. Working in batches and using damp hands, pat 1-tablespoon portions of batter into a 2-inch patty, then carefully transfer to the hot oil. Fry the bhaji for 2 to 3 minutes, until golden brown. Transfer to the prepared plate, then season to taste with salt. Repeat with the remaining batter. Serve the bhaji warm with coriander chutney.

D A R K
Twisted Spaetzle Casserole

In the German series *Dark,* generations and plotlines twist and loop back on each other. In the final moments of the third season, a small group of characters are together at a dinner party. In this moment, viewers can begin to imagine what might have happened if H.G. Tannhaus had not built his quantum machine.

To sustain you through all three seasons of this tangled and suspenseful series, you will need homemade spaetzle, a twisty German egg noodle that doubles back as often as *Dark*'s complex plot. Luckily, it's a crowd pleaser, blanketed with caramelized onions, tangy sauerkraut, lots of gooey cheese, and a generous showering of mustardy bread crumbs.

YIELD: 4 servings
PREP TIME: 30 minutes
COOK TIME: 1 hour 15 minutes

SPAETZLE

2¼ cups all-purpose flour

1 teaspoon salt, plus more for boiling

Freshly ground black pepper

3 large eggs

¾ cup whole milk

1 tablespoon unsalted butter

CARAMELIZED ONIONS

2 large onions

1 tablespoon unsalted butter

2 tablespoons olive oil

½ teaspoon granulated sugar

Kosher salt and freshly ground black pepper

CASSEROLE

Unsalted butter for greasing

½ cup dry bread crumbs

1 tablespoon spicy German mustard or Dijon mustard

1 tablespoon olive oil

Kosher salt

1 small bunch fresh dill (about ½ ounce)

8 ounces sauerkraut, drained

12 ounces Jarlsberg or Emmental cheese, coarsely grated

2 ounces Gruyère cheese, coarsely grated

1 **To make the spaetzle:** In a medium bowl, add the flour, 1 teaspoon of salt, and a few grinds of pepper, then whisk to combine. Make a well in the dry ingredients, then add the eggs and milk. Whisk the ingredients to combine, forming a soft batter.

2 Bring a large pot of salted water to a boil. Rub the butter around the sides of a medium bowl, then leave any remaining butter at the bottom.

3 Working over the boiling water, press ⅓ cup of the spaetzle batter through the large holes of a box grater, using a rubber spatula. Stir the spaetzle to break them apart, then cook for about 2 minutes, until tender. Use a slotted spoon to transfer the cooked spaetzle to the buttered bowl. Stir to coat the spaetzle in butter. Repeat with the remaining batter. (Spaetzle can be held at room temperature for about 2 hours or refrigerated overnight.)

4 **To caramelize the onions:** Peel, halve, and thinly slice the onions crosswise. In a large skillet, heat the butter and olive oil over medium until the butter melts. Add the onions to the skillet, then cook over medium heat, stirring occasionally, for about 25 minutes, until deeply browned. (Reduce the heat to medium-low if the onions are browning too quickly.) Sprinkle the onions with the sugar and a pinch each of salt and pepper. Cook for 1 to 2 minutes, until the sugar has dissolved. Remove from the heat.

5 **To assemble the casserole:** Preheat the oven to 400°F/204°C with a rack in the center position. Butter a 2-quart baking dish. In a small bowl, combine the bread crumbs, mustard, and olive oil. Season with a pinch of salt, then stir until the crumbs are evenly moistened. Coarsely chop the dill fronds and stems, then reserve 1 tablespoon for garnishing.

6 Place half of the spaetzle in the bottom of the baking dish. Top with half of the onions, sauerkraut, cheeses, and dill. Repeat with the remaining spaetzle, onions, sauerkraut, cheeses, and dill. Top with the bread crumbs.

7 Transfer the spaetzle casserole to the oven, then bake for 10 to 15 minutes, until the bread crumbs have browned and the casserole is bubbling around the edges.

8 Let the casserole stand for 5 minutes, then sprinkle with the reserved dill.

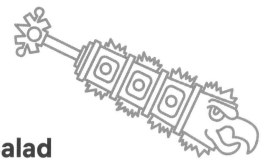

Tomato, Corn & Avocado Salad

In the animated special event *Maya and the Three*, Princess Maya wants to be more than a diplomat like her mother—she wants to fight. When Zatz, the bat prince, tries to take Maya to her coronation to the underworld to be sacrificed, her father and brothers declare that they will go to war with the gods to save her. Over the course of the story, Maya realizes her destiny as an eagle warrior, who will fight alongside her three jaguar brothers to vanquish the gods of the underworld.

To power us through Jorge Gutierrez's feast for the eyes, we created this fresh and hearty salad using staples of Mesoamerican cuisine: charred fresh corn, juicy tomatoes, and creamy avocado with just enough lime, chile, cilantro, and cotija cheese to bring everything together. You may typically use tortilla chips for scooping up dips, but we love them with a crispy, salty crouton-like addition.

YIELD: 4 servings   **PREP TIME:** 20 minutes   **COOK TIME:** 15 minutes

 VEGETARIAN   **GLUTEN FREE**

Vegetable oil for greasing

4 ears fresh corn

1 tablespoon freshly squeezed lime juice

1 garlic clove, finely chopped

¼ teaspoon granulated sugar

3 tablespoons extra virgin olive oil

Kosher salt and freshly ground black pepper

1 small red Fresno chile or jalapeño

2 ripe avocados

2 cups salted corn tortilla chips

1 pint grape tomatoes, halved

1 small bunch fresh cilantro (about ½ ounce), coarsely chopped

2 ounces cotija cheese, crumbled

1 Lightly brush a grill or grill pan with vegetable oil, then place over high heat. Remove the husks and silks from the ears of corn, then transfer the corn to the grill or grill pan. Cook, turning occasionally, for 8 to 10 minutes, until the corn is tender and charred in spots.

2 Remove the corn from the grill, then let rest for 5 to 10 minutes, until cool enough to handle. Using a sharp knife, cut the kernels off the cob, then discard the cobs.

3 In a large bowl, combine the lime juice, garlic, and sugar, and whisk until the sugar dissolves. In a slow, steady stream, whisk in the olive oil, then season the dressing to taste with salt and pepper.

4 Remove the stem and seeds from the chile, then finely chop (half or all, depending on your heat preference). Halve the avocados, remove the pit and peel, then cut into 1-inch pieces. Using your hands, break the tortilla chips into bite-sized pieces.

5 To the bowl with the dressing, add the tomatoes, chile, avocados, and two-thirds of the cilantro, cotija cheese, and chips, then stir to combine. Season to taste with salt and pepper. Garnish the salad with the remaining cilantro, cheese, and chips.

WATCH
MAYA AND THE THREE

HEARTSTOPPER

Heartwarming Fish-and-Chips

In the first season's final episode of *Heartstopper*, Nick surprises Charlie with a Sunday trip to the beach. Navigating teenage love truly leaves one hungry, so the pair get fish-and-chips, with Nick trying to catch a few of the hot chips in their mouth.

A day trip to an English beach with your special someone may not be in your immediate future, but that's no reason to delay making our version of this classic British staple.

YIELD: 4 servings
PREP TIME: 30 minutes
COOK TIME: 45 minutes

WATCH
HEARTSTOPPER

NETFLIX

Vegetable oil for frying

2 pounds russet potatoes

1½ cups beer, preferably an English bitter or lager

1½ cups all-purpose flour

Kosher salt and freshly ground black pepper

¼ cup cornstarch

Four 4- to 5-ounce haddock or cod filets

Malt vinegar for serving

Ketchup for serving

1 In a large pot or Dutch oven, heat 4 inches of vegetable oil over high until it reaches 250°F/121°C on a deep-fry thermometer. Scrub the potatoes, then cut lengthwise into ½-inch fries. Line a rimmed baking sheet with paper towels.

2 Add half of the potatoes to the oil. Cook, stirring occasionally, for about 10 minutes, until the potatoes are tender. Using a slotted spoon or spider, transfer the potatoes to the prepared baking sheet in an even layer. Repeat with the remaining potatoes, then heat the oil to 350°F/177°C.

3 Meanwhile, preheat the oven to 200°F/93°C. Set a wire rack over a rimmed baking sheet. In a large shallow bowl, add the beer and flour, whisking until smooth. Season with a pinch each of salt and pepper. Sprinkle the cornstarch on a plate. Season the fish filets all over with ¾ teaspoon of salt and a few grinds of pepper.

4 When the oil temperature reaches 350°F/177°C, add two filets to the cornstarch, turning to coat. Shake off the excess, then dip the fish into the beer batter. Lift the filets one at a time out of the batter, letting the excess drip back into the bowl. Carefully transfer to the hot oil. Fry the fish, turning once, for about 4 minutes per side, until golden brown and cooked through. Remove to the wire rack, then season with salt. Repeat with the remaining fish. Transfer the fish to the oven to keep warm.

5 Return half of the blanched fries to the oil, then fry for 4 to 5 minutes, until golden brown and crispy. Transfer to the wire rack with the fish, then season generously with salt. Repeat with the remaining fries.

6 Serve your fish-and-chips, wrapped in newspaper if you like, sprinkled with plenty of malt vinegar and with ketchup for dipping.

YOUNG ROYALS

Vegan Swedish "Meatballs" with Spaghetti

Young Royals is a Swedish coming-of-age series that centers around Prince Wilhelm (Edvin Ryding). When he arrives at the prestigious boarding school Hillerska, he gets the opportunity to find out what kind of life he really wants. Wilhelm starts dreaming of a future filled with freedom and unconditional love far away from the royal obligations. But when he unexpectedly becomes next in line for the throne, his dilemma is heightened as he has to make a choice—being in love with Simon or continuing to do his duty.

This gripping Swedish teen drama requires sustenance to survive the emotional ups and downs of the series. To get in the proper Scandinavian spirit, we suggest making this hearty vegan Swedish "meatballs" with creamy mushroom gravy, spaghetti, and lots of chopped parsley. Serve with a dollop of lingonberry jam, if you like.

YIELD: 4 servings
PREP TIME: 45 minutes
COOK TIME: 50 minutes

VEGAN

"MEATBALLS"

1 medium bunch fresh parsley (about 1 ounce), divided

2 tablespoons ground flaxseeds

¼ cup water

Two 15-ounce cans lentils

⅔ cup unsweetened oat milk

2 teaspoons kosher salt, plus more for seasoning

3 slices white sandwich bread, crusts removed

2 garlic cloves, finely chopped

⅓ cup vegan Parmesan

1 teaspoon Dijon mustard

¼ teaspoon freshly ground black pepper

¼ teaspoon ground allspice

¼ teaspoon freshly grated nutmeg

¾ cup dry bread crumbs

2 to 3 tablespoons olive oil

GRAVY

8 ounces cremini mushrooms, cleaned and stemmed

1 tablespoon olive oil, plus more for drizzling

Kosher salt and freshly ground black pepper

1 garlic clove, finely chopped

1 shallot, finely chopped

3 tablespoons vegan butter

3 tablespoons all-purpose flour

¼ teaspoon smoked paprika

2 cups vegetable stock

1½ tablespoons vegetarian Worcestershire sauce

1 tablespoon soy sauce

1 teaspoon Dijon mustard

1 cup vegan cream

1 pound spaghetti

Lingonberry jam for serving (optional)

>>recipe continues on the next page

>>Vegan Swedish Meatballs continued

1 **To make the meatballs:** Finely chop half of the parsley. In a small bowl, combine the flaxseeds with the water, then let stand for about 5 minutes, until the flaxseeds absorb the water. Drain the lentils, then measure out 2 cups (save any remaining lentils for your own use).

2 In a shallow bowl, combine the oat milk and a pinch of salt. Working one slice at a time, dip a slice of bread in the oat milk, turning to help the bread absorb the milk. Squeeze out the excess milk, then transfer to a cutting board. Repeat with the remaining slices. Cut the bread into ¼-inch cubes. Place the cubes in a medium bowl.

3 To the bowl with the bread, add the garlic, finely chopped parsley, flaxseed mixture, lentils, 2 teaspoons of the salt, vegan Parmesan, mustard, pepper, allspice, and nutmeg. Stir to combine, then add ½ cup of the bread crumbs. Using your hands, gently knead the mixture to combine. The meatball mixture should easily squeeze together into a ball. If it seems too crumbly or sticky, add more bread crumbs, 2 tablespoons at a time, until the desired consistency is achieved.

4 Preheat the oven to 350°F/177°C. Line a rimmed baking sheet with parchment paper. Using damp hands, roll the lentil mixture into 2-tablespoon balls. Place them on the prepared baking sheet as you go. Transfer the meatballs to the freezer, then chill for 5 to 10 minutes, until firm (but not frozen).

5 In a large nonstick skillet, heat 1 tablespoon of oil over medium. Working in batches, add the meatballs to the skillet, then cook for 5 to 7 minutes, until browned all over. Return them to the same baking sheet, then repeat with the remaining meatballs, adding more oil as needed. (Reserve the skillet for step 7.) After the meatballs are browned, transfer to the center rack of the oven and bake for about 8 minutes, until cooked through. Remove from the oven and cover to keep warm.

6 **To make the gravy:** Bring a large pot of salted water to a boil. Thinly slice the mushroom caps.

7 In the reserved skillet, heat 1 tablespoon of olive oil over medium-high. Add the mushrooms to the skillet, then season with salt and pepper. Cook for about 5 minutes, until the mushrooms are lightly browned and tender. Add the garlic, shallot, and a drizzle of olive oil, then cook for about 2 minutes, until the shallot has softened.

8 In the same skillet, melt the vegan butter over medium heat. Sprinkle in the flour, then cook, stirring, for 1 minute. Add the smoked paprika and vegetable stock. Bring to a brisk simmer, stirring constantly to keep the gravy smooth. Add the Worcestershire sauce, soy sauce, mustard, and vegan cream, then reduce the heat to medium-low. Cook, stirring occasionally, for about 3 minutes, until the sauce is just thick enough to coat the back of a spoon. Season the gravy to taste with salt and pepper.

9 Add the meatballs to the gravy, then cover and keep warm over low heat while the spaghetti cooks.

10 Transfer the spaghetti to the boiling water, then cook according to package directions, stirring occasionally, until it is al dente. Reserve ⅓ cup of the pasta water, then drain the spaghetti.

11 Return the spaghetti, pasta water, and ⅔ cup of the gravy to the large pot. Cook over medium heat, stirring, until the gravy coats the spaghetti.

12 Transfer the spaghetti to a large serving bowl, then spoon the meatballs and gravy over the top. Coarsely chop the remaining parsley, then sprinkle it over the top. Serve the meatballs, gravy, and spaghetti with lingonberry jam on the side, if desired.

THE RANCH

Denver Steak and Mushrooms

When Colt Bennett returns home on *The Ranch*, he visits his mom's bar with his brother, Rooster, and dad, Beau. While Beau may not think much of his son's UGG boots or his football prospects, we think the whole family would agree that Denver steaks with a creamy, whiskey-spiked mushroom sauce are incredibly delicious.

Cut from the chuck, Denver steaks are marbled and have a full, beefy flavor. Here, we pan-sear the steaks, then build a rich mushroom sauce right in the pan. For this recipe, we tip a cowboy hat to the classic steak Diane by deglazing the skillet with your choice of whiskey instead of the classic Cognac. If you would prefer not to use whiskey, you can deglaze the pan with water or chicken broth instead.

YIELD: 4 servings
PREP TIME: 15 minutes
COOK TIME: 20 minutes

WATCH THE RANCH

NETFLIX

Four 8-ounce Denver steaks

2 teaspoons kosher salt

1 teaspoon freshly ground
black pepper

1 teaspoon smoked paprika

8 ounces white button mushrooms,
cleaned and stemmed

2 tablespoons vegetable oil,
divided

1 garlic clove, finely chopped

1 shallot, finely chopped

2 tablespoons unsalted butter

2 sprigs fresh thyme

⅓ cup whiskey

⅓ cup low-sodium chicken broth

1 tablespoon Dijon mustard

1 tablespoon Worcestershire
sauce

½ cup heavy cream

1 Place the steaks on a plate. In a small bowl, thoroughly combine the salt, pepper, and smoked paprika. Season the steaks all over with the seasoning rub, then let stand at room temperature for 30 minutes.

2 Thinly slice the mushroom caps. Set aside. In a large cast-iron skillet, heat 1 tablespoon of vegetable oil over high heat. Transfer the steaks to the skillet, then cook for 2 to 3 minutes per side, until deeply browned and medium-rare. (Alternatively cook for 3½ minutes per side for medium, 5 minutes per side for well done.) Transfer the steaks to a cutting board to rest.

3 To the same skillet, add the garlic, shallot, thyme, and the remaining 1 tablespoon of vegetable oil, then reduce the heat to medium-high. Cook for about 2 minutes, until the shallot is softened. Add the mushrooms and butter, then season with salt and pepper. Cook for 5 to 6 minutes, until the mushrooms are browned and tender.

4 Remove the skillet from the heat and carefully add the whiskey. Return the skillet to medium-high heat, then cook for about 2 minutes, until the whiskey is reduced by two-thirds.

5 To the same skillet, add the broth, mustard, Worcestershire sauce, and cream. Cook, stirring occasionally, for 3 to 4 minutes, until the sauce is thick enough to coat the back of a spoon. Season the sauce to taste with salt and pepper.

6 Slice the steaks against the grain, then spoon the mushroom sauce over the top.

NARCOS
MEXICO

Michelada Chili Cocktail

In the gripping series *Narcos: Mexico*, both the drug cartels and the agents who try to stop them often enjoy a cold beer or whiskey. The perfect cocktail pairing for this series would definitely need to involve both. Enter our version of the classic Michelada. Here we use fresh lime juice, Mexican hot sauce, and a vegan Worcestershire sauce with a little agave nectar to balance the flavors, both fresh jalapeño and a pinch of chili powder are included for an extra kick. Add a little blended Scotch, a salted rim, a slice of fresh chile, and the cold beer of your choice, and you are ready to stream the next episode.

YIELD: 2 cocktails
PREP TIME: 15 minutes

 VEGAN

Kosher salt

2 limes, quartered

1 jalapeño, sliced crosswise

2 teaspoons agave nectar

4 teaspoons Mexican hot sauce

2 teaspoons vegan Worcestershire sauce

Pinch of dark chili powder

1 ounce blended Scotch, preferably Buchanan's

2 bottles Mexican beer, such as Modelo Especial or Tecate, chilled

1 Sprinkle some salt on a small plate. Rub a lime quarter around the rim of each of two pint-sized glasses. Dip the glass rims in the salt, then drop each lime wedge into the bottom of the glasses. Squeeze the remaining lime quarters into a cocktail shaker.

2 To the cocktail shaker, add half of the sliced jalapeño, agave nectar, hot sauce, Worcestershire sauce, chili powder, and Scotch. Fill the shaker with ice, then shake for about 30 seconds, until the outside feels cold. Strain into the two prepared glasses.

3 Top each glass up with the cold beer, then add ice to fill the glasses. Garnish with a slice or two of the remaining jalapeño.

SQUID GAME

Ready to watch—or rewatch—your favorite episodes of *Squid Game*? What other deadly games are our beloved characters in for? Get ready to find out. Gather your friends and throw an epic viewing party with these entertaining décor suggestions, activity ideas, recipes, and more!

▶ WATCH PARTY PLANNING

WATCH PARTY PLANNING

If you want to survive (or win) the game and throw the best *Squid Game* watch party ever, make sure to take a peek at some of the décor, activity, and recipe suggestions before your guests arrive. Don't have too much fun, however, as the guards are watching . . .

▶ Setting the Scene

Please make your way toward the game hall— or wherever the party is located—and get ready for the first set of watch party ideas.

- **Costume**: Ask your guests to come dressed in their best track suit or workout outfit, similar to the ones the players wear in the show.

- **Craft**: Create masks based on the guards from the show with black and white construction paper. Have at least 1 circle, 1 triangle, and 1 square shape accounted for.

- **Décor**: If you have the space, remove your furniture in the room where you are hosting your watch party, so that your space is as minimal as possible and there is an open area in the middle. If you have the materials, create simple "forts" or "bunkers" on the outside perimeter of your party space. These can act as your "home bases" to stream the series.

- **Décor**: If an outside space is available to you, head outside to play some of the activities on page 109.

▶ Pause & Play

- **Red Light, Green Light**: Play a friendly game of Red Light, Green Light with your guests. But instead of a giant doll that may shoot lasers at you if you move, you could instruct everyone that moves to take a Red Light, Green Light gelatin shot from page 116.

- **Dalgona Candy**: Create the dalgona candy from page 113. When your guests arrive, give everyone a small pin or a butter knife. (Always be careful when handling sharp objects!) Have each guest use a pin or knife to remove the shape from the candy. The first one that is able to remove the shape from the candy cleanly, wins!

- **Game Time**: Play some classic games with your guests, like Hopscotch or Tug of War. Be inspired by the players in the competitions featured on the show and take it very seriously—but, you know, without the "falling to your doom" part.

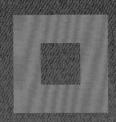

Steak Toasts

In the opening episode of *Squid Game*, Gi-hun scrambles to buy a gift and pull together a birthday dinner for his daughter, Ga-yeong. An elegant canapé, these steak toasts feature slices of bulgogi-style marinated steak draped on crispy baguette toasts with a schmear of rich compound butter, kimchi, and scallions. This recipe can be served alongside the more humble tteokbokki, page 112.

YIELD: 12 toasts (serves 4 people)
PREP TIME: 20 minutes, plus 4 hours marinating
COOK TIME: 30 minutes

STEAK MARINADE

1 small Asian or Bosc pear

2 large garlic cloves, peeled and finely chopped

¼-inch slice fresh ginger, peeled and finely chopped

3 tablespoons soy sauce

1½ tablespoons dark brown sugar

1 tablespoon mirin

1 tablespoon toasted sesame oil

Freshly ground black pepper

One 16-ounce rib eye steak

KIMCHI SCALLION BUTTER

2 tablespoons kimchi, plus ½ cup for serving

4 scallions, divided

4 tablespoons unsalted butter, softened

Pinch of kosher salt

TOASTS

1 baguette

Vegetable oil for brushing

Kosher salt and freshly ground black pepper

Toasted or black sesame seeds for garnishing

1 **To marinate the steak:** Cut the pear in half, then coarsely grate one half on the large holes of a box grater down to the core. (Discard the core and save the remaining half for your own use.) In a medium bowl, combine the garlic, ginger, grated pear, soy sauce, brown sugar, mirin, and sesame oil. Season with a few grinds of fresh pepper, then whisk to combine.

2 Pat the steak dry, then transfer to the marinade, turning to coat. Cover the bowl with plastic wrap and refrigerate for at least 4 hours, or overnight. Let the steak and marinade stand at room temperature for 30 minutes before cooking.

3 **To season the butter:** Finely chop the 2 tablespoons of kimchi and 2 of the scallions. Place the kimchi, chopped scallions, butter, and salt in a medium bowl, then stir to combine. Set aside until ready to assemble the toasts. (The butter can be refrigerated in a covered container for 2 days. Allow to soften at room temperature before proceeding with the recipe.)

4 **To bake the toasts:** Preheat the oven to 350°F/177°C with a rack in the center position. Cutting at a slight angle, cut the baguette into twelve ½-inch slices (save any remaining baguette for your own use). Arrange the slices in a single layer on a rimmed baking sheet, then brush both sides of the slices with vegetable oil. Season with salt and pepper.

5 Transfer the baguettes to the oven and bake for about 10 minutes, flipping the slices halfway through, until lightly toasted.

6 **To grill the steak:** Brush the grill grates or a grill pan with vegetable oil, then preheat with high heat (450°F/232°C on a gas grill). Place the steak on a plate, scraping off any marinade with a rubber spatula. Season it all over with salt and pepper. Transfer the seasoned steak to the grill or grill pan and reduce the heat to medium-high (400°F/204°C). Cook the steak until deeply browned and cooked to desired doneness, 6 to 8 minutes per side for medium-rare. Transfer the steak to a cutting board and let rest for 5 minutes.

7 **To assemble the toasts:** Thinly slice the remaining 2 scallions. Thinly slice the steak against the grain. Spread a generous amount of the kimchi-scallion butter on each of the toasts. Top each toast with a piece of kimchi and a slice or two of steak, then drizzle with some of the steak juices from the cutting board. Garnish with the sliced scallions and sesame seeds.

Tteokbokki

During her birthday dinner in the first episode of *Squid Game*, Ga-yeong assures her dad, Gi-hun, that she likes tteokbokki more than the steak she had earlier. Our tteokbokki recipe is cozy, spicy, and deeply comforting. Chewy rice cakes are simmered in a spicy sauce along with tender chopped cabbage and thinly sliced scallions. Perfect for a birthday celebration or a *Squid Game* viewing party!

YIELD: 4 servings
PREP TIME: 10 minutes, plus 15 minutes soaking
COOK TIME: 25 minutes

1 pound Korean rice cakes

1 tablespoon instant dashi

½ small head green cabbage (about 8 ounces)

5 scallions, divided

1 garlic clove, finely chopped

2 teaspoons gochujang

2 tablespoons granulated sugar

2 to 3 teaspoons gochugaru

1 tablespoon soy sauce

1 tablespoon toasted sesame seeds

1 teaspoon toasted sesame oil

½ teaspoon rice wine vinegar

1 Break the rice cakes apart, then rinse under cold water. Transfer to a medium bowl, then soak in hot water for 15 minutes.

2 In a large liquid measuring cup, add the dashi and 3 cups of boiling water. Whisk until the dashi is dissolved. Remove the core from the cabbage, then chop the leaves into 1-inch pieces. Cut 3 of the scallions into 1-inch pieces, then thinly slice the remaining 2.

3 In a small bowl, combine the garlic, 2 teaspoons of the gochujang, sugar, gochugaru, and soy sauce. Stir to combine. Taste, then add a little extra gochugaru, ½ teaspoon at a time, for extra heat, if desired.

4 In a medium pot, bring the dashi to a boil over high heat. To the same pot, whisk in the gochujang sauce until it has dissolved into the broth. Add the rice cakes to the boiling broth. Cook, stirring occasionally, for 4 to 6 minutes, until the rice cakes are chewy and tender. (Check the recommended cooking time on the rice cake package as well.)

5 Add the chopped cabbage and 1-inch scallion pieces to the same pot. Reduce the heat to medium, then cook, stirring occasionally, for about 3 minutes, until the cabbage is tender and the sauce has thickened slightly.

6 Remove the pot from the heat. Stir in the sesame seeds, sesame oil, and vinegar. Garnish with the thinly sliced scallions.

Perfectly Stamped Dalgona Candy

In an episode of *Squid Game*, the players are brought to line up behind one of four shapes: a circle, star, triangle, and umbrella. During the game, known as ppopgi, the players must carefully remove the shape from the dalgona (a Korean honeycomb candy) surrounding it without breaking the shape in 10 minutes. If the clock runs out or the shape is broken, they lose.

The candy is most often made by melting sugar in a metal ladle over a flame and then quickly pressing and stamping the candy. In our recipe inspired by the show, we use a small saucepan to melt the sugar, allowing you to make all four candies at once. Before you begin, make sure you have all of your equipment out, organized, and within easy reach. The recipe goes quickly once it starts! Thanks in part to the huge popularity of *Squid Game*, you can now purchase silicone dalgona molds. If you choose to use a mold, lightly spray the mold in step 1 and move on to step 3.

YIELD: 4 pieces of candy   **PREP TIME:** 10 minutes   **COOK TIME:** 10 minutes

VEGETARIAN   **GLUTEN FREE**

2 teaspoons vegetable oil

½ cup granulated sugar

3 tablespoons honey

¼ teaspoon baking soda

1 Line a rimmed baking sheet with parchment paper, then drizzle with the oil. Using your hands, coat the parchment evenly with the oil. Generously grease four cookie cutters with more vegetable oil (2- to 3-inch cookie cutters will work best).

2 In a small saucepan, combine the sugar and the honey. Place the saucepan on the stove top.

3 Heat the sugar and honey mixture over medium-low, stirring carefully and occasionally with a rubber spatula or chopstick, for 8 to 10 minutes, until the sugar has melted and the mixture is golden brown and just a little darker than light brown sugar. Once the mixture starts to get brown in spots, you can swirl the pan gently to even out the color.

4 Add the baking soda, gently stirring to combine. Remove the saucepan from the heat.

5 Working quickly, pour the mixture into four equal circles. (It is okay if the circles aren't perfectly round.) Let the caramel cool for 1 minute, then stamp with the cookie cutters. (Stamping each shape several times in a row will make it easier to separate the shape from the surrounding candy.)

6 Let cool completely for about 10 minutes before eating or trying to remove the center shape.

Bibimbap

During the course of *Squid Game*, the participants are given simple meals that might be fed to a child: bento boxes with fried eggs, rice, kimchi, and vegetable banchan; sweet soboro bun with peanut streusel; a boiled egg and a bottle of cider. The bento boxes served to contestants have many of the bibimbap components: fried eggs, kimchi, rice, and vegetables. Although bibimbap is often made with beef, we were inspired by the contents of the old-fashioned school lunch box contents and made ours without.

YIELD: 4 servings
PREP TIME: 25 minutes
COOK TIME: 45 minutes

 VEGETARIAN

2 cups sushi rice
2 cups water
1 teaspoon kosher salt

SAUTÉED CARROTS

2 medium carrots, peeled with ends trimmed
2 teaspoons vegetable oil
2 scallions, thinly sliced
2 teaspoons rice vinegar
1 teaspoon soy sauce
Freshly ground black pepper

SEASONED SOYBEAN SPROUTS

8 ounces soybean sprouts
2 scallions, finely chopped
1 garlic clove, finely chopped
1½ teaspoons toasted sesame oil
¼ teaspoon gochugaru
Pinch of kosher salt

SESAME SPINACH

10 ounces fresh spinach
1 garlic clove, finely chopped
1 scallion, finely chopped
1 teaspoon soy sauce
1½ teaspoons toasted sesame oil
2 teaspoons toasted sesame seeds
1 tablespoon vegetable oil
4 large eggs
Kosher salt and freshly ground black pepper
Gochujang for serving
Kimchi for serving

1 **To make the rice:** In a medium saucepan, combine the rice, water, and salt. Bring to a boil, then cover, reduce the heat to low, and cook for about 15 minutes, until the rice is tender and the water has been absorbed. Remove from the heat, then keep covered to keep warm until ready to serve.

2 **To make the sautéed carrots:** Cut the carrots in half lengthwise, then thinly slice into half-moons. In a large nonstick skillet, heat the oil over medium-high. Add the carrots and scallions to the skillet, then cook for 3 to 4 minutes, until the carrots are just crisp-tender. Add the vinegar, soy sauce, and a few grinds of pepper to the skillet and cook for 1 minute more. Transfer to a medium bowl. Wipe out the skillet and reserve for step 6.

3 **To make the seasoned soybean sprouts:** Bring a large saucepan half full of salted water to a boil. Add the soybean sprouts, then cook for about 3 minutes, until crisp-tender. Drain, then rinse with cold water. (Reserve the saucepan for step 4.) Transfer to a medium bowl and add the scallions and garlic. Add the sesame oil, gochugaru, and salt to the same bowl. Stir to combine.

4 **To make the sesame spinach:** Half fill the same saucepan with water, then season with salt and bring to a boil. Wash the spinach in cold water to remove any sand or grit, then trim off thick stems. Add the spinach to the boiling water, then cook for about 30 seconds, until just wilted. Drain the spinach, then rinse with cold water to stop the cooking. Squeeze out all of the liquid, then transfer to a medium bowl.

5 Add the garlic and scallion to the spinach. To the same bowl, add the soy sauce, toasted sesame oil, and sesame seeds, then stir to combine.

6 **To fry the eggs:** In the reserved nonstick skillet, heat the oil over medium. Crack all 4 eggs into the skillet, then season with salt and pepper. Cook for 1 to 2 minutes, until the whites are just set. Cover and cook for about 1 minute, until the yolks are just set.

7 **To assemble the bibimbap:** Uncover the rice, then fluff with a fork. Divide it among four bowls, then top with the carrots, bean sprouts, spinach, and fried eggs. Serve with gochujang and kimchi.

Red Light, Green Light Soju Gelatin Shots

Red Light, Green Light may be a classic children's game, but in the show *Squid Game*, this iconic contest shows the contestants the swift and brutal consequences of losing. Flavored with fresh fruit juices and just enough soju to make you take notice, these bite-sized treats are the perfect cocktail for a *Squid Game* marathon. You can add a drop of red and green food coloring to make the shots more vibrant or go without for a slightly more natural hue. These gelatin shots can also be made with gin or vodka. For a nonalcoholic version, substitute lemon-lime soda or ginger ale for the soju.

YIELD: 24 gelatin shots
PREP TIME: 30 minutes, plus 90 minutes for chilling
COOK TIME: 10 minutes

RED BERRY SOJU GELATIN SHOTS

7 medium fresh strawberries (about 6 ounces)

1 cup fresh raspberries (about 4 ounces), divided

3 tablespoons pomegranate juice

2 tablespoons granulated sugar

Red food coloring (optional)

2¼ teaspoons unflavored gelatin

3 tablespoons soju

HONEYDEW AND GREEN GRAPE SOJU GELATIN SHOTS

1 lime

¼ of a small ripe honeydew melon (about 12 ounces), cut into 1-inch cubes

1 cup seedless green grapes (about 6 ounces), divided

2 tablespoons of water

1 tablespoon granulated sugar

1 tablespoon honey

Green food coloring (optional)

2¼ teaspoons unflavored gelatin

3 tablespoons soju

116

1 Lightly coat one 24-cup mini-muffin pan with nonstick baking spray. Set aside.

2 **To make the Red Berry Soju Gelatin Shots:** Trim the tops off the strawberries, then place the strawberries in a blender, along with ¾ cup of the raspberries and the pomegranate juice. Blend until very smooth. Pour the puree through a fine-mesh strainer, using a spoon to press on the solids. This should make about ¾ cup of juice.

3 Transfer the berry juice to a small saucepan and add the sugar. Add a drop of red food coloring, if you want a more vivid color. Sprinkle the gelatin over the top. Let stand for about 5 minutes, until the gelatin has softened and absorbed some of the liquid.

4 Place the saucepan on the stove top. Heat over low, whisking occasionally, for about 5 minutes, until the mixture is warm and both the gelatin and sugar have dissolved. (Do not allow the liquid to boil.) Remove from the heat and stir in the soju.

5 Cut the remaining ¼ cup of raspberries in half and place one half in each of 12 mini-muffin cups. Carefully pour the berry mixture into a heatproof liquid measuring cup, then divide it evenly among 12 muffin cups.

6 Carefully transfer the pan to the refrigerator and chill for about 90 minutes, until firm.

7 **To make the Honeydew & Green Grape Soju Gelatin Shots:** Finely grate ½ teaspoon of lime zest, then squeeze 1 teaspoon of juice into a small bowl. In a blender, combine the honeydew melon, ¾ cup of the grapes, and water. Blend until very smooth. Pour the puree through a fine-mesh strainer, using a spoon to press on the solids. This should make about ¾ cup of juice.

8 Transfer the honeydew mixture to a small saucepan, then whisk in the lime zest and juice, sugar, and honey. Add a drop of green food coloring, if you want a more vivid color. Sprinkle the gelatin over the top. Let stand for about 5 minutes, until the gelatin has softened and absorbed some of the liquid.

9 Transfer the saucepan to the stove top. Heat over low, whisking occasionally, for 2 to 3 minutes, until the mixture is warm and both the gelatin and sugar have dissolved. (Do not allow the liquid to boil.) Remove from the heat and stir in the soju.

10 Remove the muffin pan from the refrigerator. Thinly slice the remaining ¼ cup of grapes, then put a slice or two in the bottom of each of the remaining muffin cups. Carefully pour the honeydew mixture into a heatproof liquid measuring cup, then divide it evenly among the muffin cups.

11 Carefully transfer the pan to the refrigerator and chill for about 90 minutes, until firm. Just before serving, carefully unmold the soju shots and arrange on a serving platter.

▶▶ Fast forward

To create a two-toned, layered soju shot, lightly grease a 12-cup muffin tin. Divide the red berry mixture among the 12 cups, then chill for about 45 minutes, until set but still slightly sticky on top. Top with the honeydew mixture and chill for about 90 minutes, until firm.

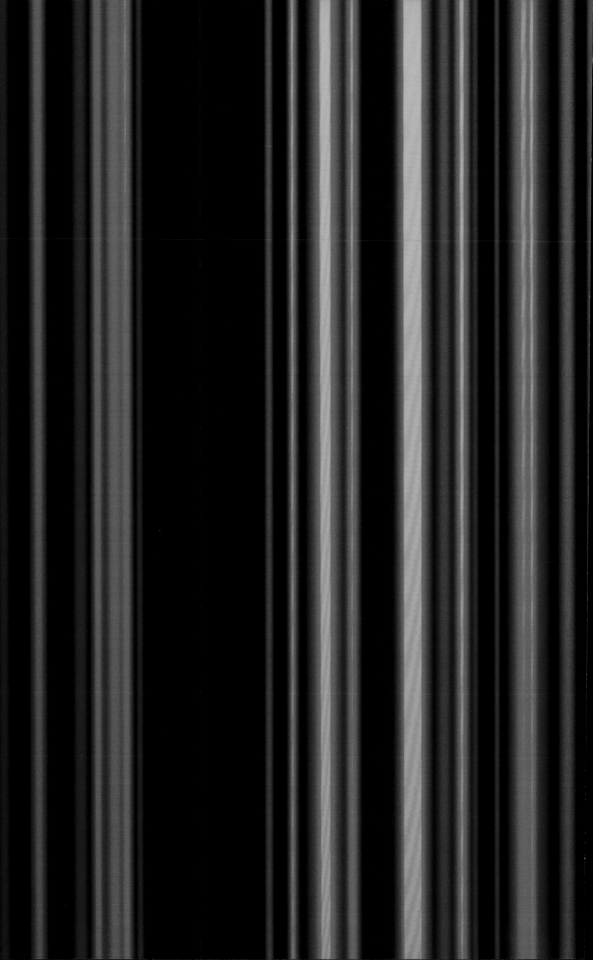

Holiday Fare

7

Enjoy any of the holidays all year
round with the festive food from your
favorite movies and shows streaming
on Netflix.

always be my Maybe

Valentine's Kimchi Jjigae Burrito

In an early scene in the film *Always Be My Maybe*, Marcus's mom, Judy, shows Sasha, his best friend, how to make kimchi jjigae. As she stirs the stew, she talks with Sasha, dropping culinary wisdom like how "we Koreans use scissors for everything— vegetables, noodles." Then she hands them to Sasha so she can snip scallions, too.

Always Be My Maybe ends just as it starts, with Marcus, Sasha, and a bubbling pot of kimchi jjigae, a dish that feels like home to both. Here, we take this comforting, spicy stew and create a truly mouthwatering burrito, a play on Marcus's request for a "monochrome burrito to go" after finding himself still hungry after a fancy meal with Sasha. The kimchi jjigae is layered with sushi rice and mild cheese, then wrapped in a flour tortilla and browned in a skillet. The perfect dinner for a cozy Netflix and Chill evening with someone who makes you feel like home.

YIELD: 4 burritos
PREP TIME: 25 minutes
COOK TIME: 1 hour

1 cup sushi rice

1 cup water

Kosher salt

1 teaspoon toasted sesame seeds

1½ cups kimchi, plus ¼ cup kimchi liquid

2 ounces shiitake mushrooms, stemmed

6 ounces extra-firm tofu (about half of package), drained

4 scallions

2 tablespoons vegetable oil, divided

4 ounces pork belly, cut into ½-inch pieces

1 garlic clove, finely chopped

2 teaspoons gochujang

1 teaspoon gochugaru

1 teaspoon granulated sugar

1 teaspoon fish sauce

½ teaspoon toasted sesame oil

1 cup low-sodium chicken broth

4 large flour tortillas

8 ounces mozzarella or mild cheddar cheese, coarsely grated

1. In a small saucepan, combine the rice, water, and ½ teaspoon of salt. Bring to a boil, then cover, reduce the heat to low, and cook for about 15 minutes, until the water has been absorbed and the rice is tender. Remove from the heat, sprinkle with the sesame seeds, then fluff the rice with a fork. Cover to keep warm.

2. Coarsely chop the kimchi, reserving ¼ cup of the liquid. (If you have less liquid, make up the difference with water.) Coarsely chop the mushroom caps. Pat the tofu dry and cut it into ½-inch cubes. Trim the ends from the scallions, then, like Judy Kim, use kitchen shears to cut them into ½-inch pieces.

3. In a medium pot, heat 1 tablespoon of oil over medium-high. Add the chopped kimchi and the pork belly to the pot. Cook, stirring occasionally, for about 6 minutes, until the kimchi has softened and the pork is cooked through. Add the mushrooms and garlic to the pot, then season with salt. Cook for about 2 minutes, until the garlic is fragrant and the mushrooms are just tender.

4. To the same pot, add the kimchi liquid, gochujang, gochugaru, sugar, fish sauce, sesame oil, and chicken broth, then stir to combine. Bring to a boil, then cook on high heat for 5 minutes.

5. Carefully stir in the tofu, then cover the pot, reduce the heat to medium, and cook for about 15 minutes, until the tofu is warm and the stew is thick and flavorful. Stir in the scallions, then season the sauce to taste with salt or more fish sauce. Remove from the heat and let cool slightly.

6. Arrange the tortillas on a work surface, then divide the rice among the tortillas, leaving a 1-inch border on all sides. Using a slotted spoon, spoon the kimchi jjigae over the rice, then top with the cheese. Fold in the sides of the tortillas, then roll up tightly.

7. In a large nonstick skillet, heat the remaining 1 tablespoon of oil over medium-high. Add the burritos, seam side down, to the skillet and cook for 2 to 3 minutes, until golden brown. Flip the burritos, then cook for 2 to 3 minutes, until golden brown on the other side. Transfer to plates and serve with extra kimchi on the side.

▶▶ Fast forward

Kimchi jjigae is often simmered in a homemade anchovy broth. Here we use chicken broth and fish sauce to approximate some of the umami flavors of the anchovy broth. Kimchi jjigae also often calls for mukeunji, an aged and fermented kimchi. It is available in many Asian grocery stores and Korean markets, but any cabbage kimchi will also be good here.

H♥LIDATE

Cinco de Mayo Paloma

In the Netflix rom-com *Holidate*, Sloane and Jackson meet at the mall in the middle of a truly lousy Christmas for both. Jackson proposes that they be each other's holidate: a fun plus-one for any holiday, no strings attached. The duo spend their fifth holidate at a Mexican restaurant with free-flowing tequila, celebrating Cinco de Mayo. And, in true rom-com tradition, things get complicated.

Instead of tequila shots, we'll be rewatching *Holidate* this Cinco de Mayo with our version of the classic paloma. Our recipe uses both grapefruit juice and grapefruit soda as well as reposado tequila, an aged tequila with a more mellow agave flavor.

YIELD: 2 cocktails
PREP TIME: 10 minutes

 VEGAN

1 lime

½ teaspoon kosher salt

½ teaspoon granulated sugar

½ cup freshly squeezed grapefruit juice

3 ounces reposado tequila

Ice

12 ounces chilled grapefruit soda

1 Finely grate ½ teaspoon of lime zest, then halve the lime. Cut one thin slice of lime, then juice the remainder. Place the lime zest, salt, and sugar on a small plate, then rub them together until the sweet-salty mixture is slightly damp. Set aside.

2 In a cocktail shaker, combine the lime juice, grapefruit juice, and tequila. Top with ice, then stir to combine.

3 Rub the rims of two highball glasses with the reserved lime slice, then dip the glasses into the lime-salt mixture. Strain the juice and tequila mixture into the glasses, then top up with the grapefruit soda and a few ice cubes.

Moon Festival Dumplings

In the animated film *Over the Moon*, Fei Fei's family shop is famous for its special mooncakes, made for the Autumn Moon Festival. When Fei Fei is first invited to help her parents, she is thrilled, happily working as the others sing "Stuff, roll, press, smack! Stuff, roll, press, smack! Sift the flour, let the eggs crack, knead the dough every hour, then we start again!"

The Autumn Moon Festival is often celebrated with duck, pomelos, buffalo nuts, crab, and Asian pears in addition to mooncakes, both savory and sweet. For our *Over the Moon* dumplings, we drew inspiration from pork mooncakes. Instead of sugar or honey, we use grated apple, a fruit whose Chinese name, ping guo, sounds like the Chinese word for peace, ping.

YIELD: 30 dumplings   **PREP TIME:** 1 hour   **COOK TIME:** 25 minutes

1 **To make the filling:** Add the apple to a medium bowl. Sprinkle with a pinch of salt. Let stand for 5 to 10 minutes, until the salt has drawn some of the moisture out of the apple. Place the apple in a clean tea towel, then squeeze out the excess moisture. Rinse the bowl, then wipe it clean. Return the apple to the bowl.

2 To the bowl with the grated apple, add the ginger, garlic, scallions, pork, wine, cornstarch, soy sauce, and sesame oil. Stir or knead with your hands to combine.

3 **To assemble the dumplings:** Line a rimmed baking sheet with parchment paper. Fill a small bowl with water. Have both your pork filling and wonton wrappers within easy reach. Working one at a time, transfer 1 tablespoon of the pork to the center of a wonton wrapper. Lightly moisten the wonton wrapper edges, then fold the wrapper in half to cover the filling. Pinch the middle of the curved side to seal, then make two folds from the center from each side, pressing on the pleats with damp fingers to help seal the dumpling. Repeat with the remaining filling. (Save any remaining wonton wrappers for your own use.)

4 **To cook the dumplings:** Heat the oil in a large nonstick skillet over medium-high. Working in batches if necessary, add the dumplings in an even layer, pleat side up. Cook for about 3 minutes, until the bottoms are browned. Carefully add ¼ cup of water, then cover and reduce the heat to low. Steam for 3 to 4 minutes, until the wrappers are nearly translucent and the filling is cooked through. Remove from the heat.

5 **To make the dipping sauce:** In a small bowl, thoroughly combine the garlic, scallion, soy sauce, vinegar, chili oil, sesame oil, and sesame seeds. Serve with the hot dumplings.

DUMPLINGS

1 small apple, preferably Pink Lady but any apple will do (about 8 ounces), peeled and coarsely grated

½ teaspoon plus a pinch kosher salt, divided

¼-inch slice fresh ginger, peeled and finely chopped

1 garlic clove, peeled and finely chopped

4 scallions, thinly sliced

8 ounces ground pork

1 tablespoon Shaoxing wine

1 teaspoon cornstarch

1½ teaspoons soy sauce

½ teaspoon sesame oil

One 12-ounce package wonton wrappers

2 tablespoons vegetable oil

DIPPING SAUCE

1 garlic clove, finely chopped

1 scallion, finely chopped

3 tablespoons soy sauce

1 tablespoon Chinkiang (black) vinegar

1 teaspoon chili oil

1 teaspoon toasted sesame oil

2 teaspoons toasted sesame seeds

WATCH
OVER THE MOON

MIDNIGHT MASS

Bleeding Angel Cake

On Crockett Island, a small fishing community, something strange is afoot. First, Monsignor Pruitt, the priest of the Catholic Church, disappears on a pilgrimage to the Holy Land, and a new priest, Father Paul Hill, arrives. Next, hundreds of dead cats appear on the beach, and the parishioners begin healing from all sorts of ailments. Rather than a miracle, these mysteries have a darker, more blood-thirsty source.

A gripping horror series like *Midnight Mass* requires a cake that really captures the spirit of the show: dark chocolate layers, creamy vanilla buttercream, and a drippy and blood-red fruit preserve filling. To finish it all off, an easy fake "blood" you can drizzle and splatter all over the outside of the cake—a showstopping center-piece for any Halloween get-together.

WATCH
MIDNIGHT MASS

YIELD: One 8-inch three-layer cake
PREP TIME: 1 hour, plus 1 hour cooling
COOK TIME: 30 minutes

 VEGETARIAN

CHOCOLATE CAKE

Nonstick cooking spray

2¼ cups all-purpose flour

1½ cups granulated sugar

1 cup plus 2 tablespoons unsweetened Dutch process cocoa powder

1 tablespoon espresso powder

1½ teaspoons kosher salt

1⅛ teaspoons baking powder

1⅛ teaspoons baking soda

½ teaspoon ground cinnamon

3 large eggs

1 cup plus 2 tablespoons buttermilk

1 cup plus 2 tablespoons hot water

¾ cup light brown sugar

1 tablespoon pure vanilla extract

¾ cup vegetable oil

VANILLA BUTTERCREAM

2 sticks unsalted butter

6 to 7 cups confectioners' sugar

¼ teaspoon kosher salt

¼ cup sour cream

1 teaspoon vanilla extract

1 cup strawberry, cherry, or seedless raspberry preserves

2 teaspoons plus 2 drops red food coloring, divided

1 tablespoon maple syrup

1 **To make the chocolate cake:** Preheat the oven to 350°F/177°C with a rack in the center position. Spray three 8-inch cake pans with nonstick spray, then line the bottom of each pan with a circle of parchment. Lightly spray the parchment. In a large bowl, add the flour, the granulated sugar, cocoa powder, espresso powder, salt, baking powder, baking soda, and ground cinnamon, then whisk to combine. Make a well in the dry ingredients, then crack the eggs into the well and whisk with a fork to break up the yolks. To the same bowl, add the buttermilk, hot water, brown sugar, vanilla, and vegetable oil. Whisk the batter until the ingredients are combined, then divide among prepared pans. Smooth the tops with a spatula.

2 Transfer the cake pans to the oven, then bake until the cake springs back lightly to the touch and a skewer inserted in the center comes out clean, 25 to 30 minutes.

3 Transfer to a wire rack, then cool for 20 minutes. Invert the cakes, then remove the parchment. Flip the cakes back so the top side is up, then cool completely, about 30 minutes more.

4 **To make the vanilla buttercream:** While the cakes are cooling, place the unsalted butter on the counter to come up to room temperature, about 45 minutes. Cut the softened butter into 1-inch pieces.

5 Using a hand mixer, beat the butter until smooth and creamy, 3 to 4 minutes. Add salt and ½ cup of the confectioners' sugar, then beat on low until the sugar has been incorporated. Add the remaining confectioners' sugar, ½ cup at a time, then add the sour cream and vanilla. Beat on medium speed until light and fluffy, 2 to 3 minutes. If the buttercream is too soft, add small amounts of powdered sugar until stiff peaks form.

6 **To assemble the cake:** In a small bowl, combine the preserves and 2 drops of red food coloring. Add more red food coloring, one drop at a time, to achieve a more vibrant red color.

7 Using a serrated knife, trim off the domed top of each layer cake. Transfer the first layer to a cake stand. Spread ¾ cup of the vanilla buttercream in an even layer across the top. Spread ½ cup of the preserves on top of the buttercream, leaving a ½-inch border around the edge. Top with the second cake layer, then spread with another ¾ cup of the buttercream and the remaining ½ cup of the preserves. Top with the third cake layer. Spread a thin layer of the frosting on the top and sides of the cake, then chill until the frosting is firm, about 15 minutes. Spread the remaining buttercream on the top and sides of the cake.

8 In a small bowl, combine the remaining 2 teaspoons of red food coloring and the maple syrup. Using a clean silicone pastry brush or a fork, splatter the cake with the fake "blood."

SANTA CLARITA DIET

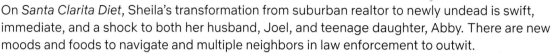

The Undead Meat Loaf

On *Santa Clarita Diet*, Sheila's transformation from suburban realtor to newly undead is swift, immediate, and a shock to both her husband, Joel, and teenage daughter, Abby. There are new moods and foods to navigate and multiple neighbors in law enforcement to outwit.

To celebrate this dark and deeply hilarious series and the Halloween season—and to make the perfect food pairing—we offer you this meat loaf take on Gary's zombie head that plagues Abby and Joel. Full of savory turkey and turkey sausage, glazed with marinara, and wrapped in prosciutto, it is sure to delight both the alive and undead.

YIELD: 4–6 servings   **PREP TIME:** 25 minutes   **COOK TIME:** 50 minutes

1 tablespoon olive oil

1 shallot, finely chopped

2 garlic cloves, finely chopped

1 red bell pepper, finely chopped

Kosher salt and freshly ground black pepper

2 large eggs

1 ounce Parmigiano Reggiano, finely grated

1 small bunch fresh parsley (about ½ ounce), finely chopped

1 pound ground turkey, preferably dark meat

1 pound spicy Italian turkey sausage, casings removed if necessary

½ cup dry bread crumbs

1 teaspoon dried oregano

2 teaspoons Worcestershire sauce

½ cup marinara sauce, plus more for serving

1 small yellow onion, peeled

2 whole cloves

2 ounces sliced prosciutto

1 **To make the meat loaf mixture:** In a medium skillet, heat the oil over medium-high. Add the shallot, garlic, and pepper to the skillet, then season with a pinch each of salt and black pepper. Cook for 3 to 4 minutes, until the pepper and shallot have softened and the garlic is fragrant. Transfer the vegetable mixture to a plate, then cool completely, for about 20 minutes.

2 Preheat the oven to 375°F/190°C with a rack in the center position. Line a rimmed baking sheet with parchment paper. In a medium bowl, whisk the eggs to combine, then add the cooled vegetables, cheese, parsley, ground turkey, turkey sausage, bread crumbs, oregano, Worcestershire sauce, and 1½ teaspoons salt. Add a few grinds of pepper, then knead lightly with your hands until just combined.

3 Transfer the mixture to the prepared baking sheet, then shape into a head. Make two indentations for the eyes and a shallow half-moon for the mouth, then spread the marinara sauce over the meat loaf.

4 Balancing the onion on the root end, cut two ¼-inch slices off of the rounded sides of the onion. Press one into each of the eye indentations, rounded side up. Press one clove into each onion slice to make the pupil. Cut some of the remaining onion into ½-inch squares to use as teeth, then make the mouth, pressing each tooth gently into the meat loaf mixture. Drizzle the onion eyes and teeth with a little olive oil.

5 Place the meat loaf in the oven and bake for about 40 minutes, until the meat loaf has browned and an instant-read thermometer inserted into the thickest part reads 165°F/74°C. Remove the meat loaf from the oven, then preheat the broiler.

6 Carefully arrange the prosciutto in slightly overlapping slices on an angle, working around the eyes and mouth.

7 Broil the meat loaf for 2 to 3 minutes, until the prosciutto is warm and browned in spots (watch closely as broilers vary). Let stand at room temperature for 5 minutes before serving. Serve the meat loaf with more warm marinara sauce on the side.

|ORANGE| is the new BLACK|

Halloween Hooch

For the first four seasons of *Orange Is the New Black*, Poussey Washington was well known in Litchfield for her homemade hooch. Because it was always shared as a gesture of goodwill or for fun, Poussey even turned down Vee's offer to sell the moonshine in season two.

Our Halloween-worthy moonshine cocktail gets its vibrant hue from orange juice and mango nectar, while ginger beer and fresh lime juice balance the sweetness.

YIELD: 2 cocktails
PREP TIME: 10 minutes

 VEGAN

Freshly squeezed juice of 1 lime

⅔ cup orange juice

½ cup mango nectar

½ cup moonshine

Ice

¾ cup ginger beer

2 thin orange slices for garnishing

WATCH ORANGE IS THE NEW BLACK

1 Add the lime juice to a cocktail shaker, then top with the orange juice, mango nectar, and moonshine. Fill the shaker with ice, then stir to combine.

2 Strain the orange juice mixture into each of two highball glasses, then top with the ginger beer. Add a few ice cubes, then garnish each glass with an orange slice.

BEST LEFTOVERS EVER!

Best Thanksgiving Leftover Lunch Ever!

Best Leftovers Ever! challenges contestants to re-create new dishes from a wide range of leftovers. For a Thanksgiving episode in season three, the three contestants made judge-pleasing sandwiches from leftover green bean casserole, ham, apple pie, and sausage stuffing.

To celebrate the show and the boundless creativity of the contestants, we turned our thoughts to Thanksgiving leftovers, too. First, we transformed leftover stuffing into crisp, cheesy waffles (stuffles?). Next, we smothered our waffles with a cozy turkey and mushroom gravy and topped it all with fried eggs. We garnished the whole thing with chopped chives and hot sauce. The cranberry sauce on the side feels more necessary than optional.

YIELD: 4 servings
PREP TIME: 20 minutes
COOK TIME: 45 minutes

STUFFING WAFFLES

2 large eggs

Kosher salt and freshly ground black pepper

8 ounces sharp cheddar cheese, coarsely grated

4½ cups leftover stuffing

Nonstick cooking spray for greasing

TURKEY & MUSHROOM GRAVY

4 ounces white button mushrooms, cleaned and stemmed

1 tablespoon olive oil

1 shallot, finely chopped

1 garlic clove, finely chopped

¼ teaspoon smoked paprika

Kosher salt and freshly ground black pepper

2 cups leftover turkey meat, torn into bite-sized pieces

½ cup low-sodium chicken broth

1 cup leftover gravy

FRIED EGGS

1 tablespoon unsalted butter

1 tablespoon olive oil

4 large eggs

Kosher salt and freshly ground pepper

1 small bunch fresh chives (about ½ ounce), finely chopped

Hot sauce for serving (optional)

Leftover cranberry sauce for serving (optional)

>>recipe continues on the next page

1 **To make the stuffing waffles:** Preheat the oven to 250°F/121°C. In a large bowl, whisk the eggs with a pinch each of salt and pepper until combined. Add the cheddar and stuffing to the bowl, then stir until combined.

2 Lightly coat a waffle iron with nonstick spray, then heat to medium-high. Place some of the stuffing mixture on the preheated waffle iron, then pat into a firm, even layer. (How much stuffing you add to each waffle will vary by the waffle iron.) Close and cook for 4 to 6 minutes, until golden brown and cooked through. Transfer the cooked waffle to a rimmed baking sheet, then place in the oven to keep warm. Repeat with the remaining stuffing mixture.

3 **To make the turkey & mushroom gravy:** Thinly slice the mushroom caps. In a medium pot, heat the oil over medium-high. Add the shallot, garlic, paprika, and a pinch each of salt and pepper to the pot, then cook for 2 to 3 minutes, until the shallot has softened. Add the mushrooms to the same pot, then season with salt and pepper. (You can add an extra tablespoon of oil if the pot seems dry.) Cook for 4 to 5 minutes, until the mushrooms are browned and tender.

4 To the same pot, stir in the turkey, chicken broth, and leftover gravy. Bring to a simmer, then reduce the heat to low, stirring occasionally, for about 5 minutes, until the turkey is warm and the gravy is thick enough to coat the back of a spoon. Season to taste with salt and pepper, then remove from heat and cover to keep warm.

5 **To fry the eggs:** In a large nonstick skillet, heat the butter and olive oil over medium-high. Crack all 4 eggs into the skillet, then season with salt and pepper. Cook for 1 to 2 minutes, until the whites are just set. Cover and cook for about 1 minute, until the yolks are just set. Transfer the eggs to a plate.

6 Top the warm waffles with the turkey and mushroom gravy and fried eggs. Garnish with the chives. Serve with hot sauce, leftover cranberry sauce, or both, if desired!

THE WITCHER

Witchmas Banquet Bourguignon

5 ounces slab bacon

2 pounds beef cheeks

1 large yellow onion, peeled

4 medium carrots
(about 1 pound), divided

3 large garlic cloves, divided

3 sprigs fresh thyme

1 medium bunch fresh parsley
(about 1 ounce), divided

3 tablespoons all-purpose flour

2 teaspoons kosher salt, plus
more for seasoning

1 teaspoon freshly ground black
pepper, plus more for seasoning

3 tablespoons olive oil, divided

1 tablespoon tomato paste

2 bay leaves

1 tablespoon Worcestershire
sauce

3 cups Pinot Noir

2 cups beef broth

4 medium shallots

2 tablespoons butter, divided

2 tablespoons olive oil, divided

8 ounces cremini mushrooms,
cleaned and quartered lengthwise

Crusty bread or buttered egg
noodles for serving

In *The Witcher*, Geralt of Rivia, a gruff monster hunter for hire, known as a witcher, is often slaying creatures of one sort or another. In the first season, he is a somewhat reluctant guest at a royal banquet Queen Calanthe threw to evaluate would-be husbands for her daughter, Princess Pavetta.

Sumptuous royal banquets, such as this one, require rich, hearty dishes. While there's more posturing and sword fighting than menu discussion in this episode, our Witchmas Banquet Bourguignon would have been just the thing to serve. French beef bourguignon can be made with chuck or even brisket, but using beef cheeks befits a magical royal banquet where a knight with the head of a hedgehog will win a powerful princess's heart.

YIELD: 4 servings
PREP TIME: 35 minutes
COOK TIME: 3 hours, 30 minutes

1 Preheat the oven to 300°F/149°C with a rack in the center position. Cut the slab bacon into ½-inch slices, then cut crosswise into ½-inch batons. Pat the beef cheeks dry, then cut into 1-inch cubes. Cut the onion into quarters, leaving the root end intact. Peel and trim the carrots. Cut 2 of the carrots in half lengthwise, then cut each in half crosswise. Cut the remaining 2 carrots into 1-inch chunks. Peel all of the garlic, then crush 2 of the cloves. Finely chop the third garlic clove, then reserve it for step 8. Using kitchen twine, tie the thyme sprigs and half of the parsley into a bundle.

2 Line a plate with paper towels. Heat a large Dutch oven over medium. Add the bacon to the Dutch oven and cook for 5 to 7 minutes, until golden brown. Using a slotted spoon, transfer the cooked bacon to the prepared plate.

3 While the bacon cooks, in a medium bowl, combine the flour, 2 teaspoons of salt, and 1 teaspoon of pepper, stirring to combine. Add the beef cheeks to the bowl, then gently toss to coat the beef.

4 Increase the heat under the Dutch oven to medium-high. Working in batches, add the beef cheeks, and cook them for 8 to 10 minutes, until deeply browned on all sides. Transfer the browned beef to a plate, then repeat with the remaining meat.

>>recipe continues on the next page

>>Witchmas Banquet Bourguignon continued

5 To the Dutch oven, add the onion quarters, carrot halves, crushed garlic, and 1 tablespoon of the olive oil. Season with salt and pepper. Cook, scraping the browned bits, for 3 to 4 minutes, until the vegetables are lightly browned. Add the tomato paste and cook for about 2 minutes, until the paste is slightly darker.

6 Add the beef and any juices, the herb bundles, bay leaves, Worcestershire sauce, Pinot Noir, and beef broth. Bring to a simmer, then cover. Transfer to the oven and braise for about 2½ hours, until the beef is very tender. Meanwhile, peel the shallots, then quarter lengthwise, leaving the root end intact.

7 In a large skillet, heat 1 tablespoon each of the butter and olive oil over medium-high until the butter melts. Add the carrots chunks and shallots to the skillet, then season with salt and pepper. Cook for 5 to 7 minutes, until the vegetables are tender. Transfer to a medium bowl, then return the skillet to the stove top. Heat the remaining 1 tablespoon each of butter and olive oil, then add the mushrooms. Season with salt and pepper, then cook for about 5 minutes, until the mushrooms are browned and tender. Transfer to the bowl with the carrots and shallots.

8 Finely chop the remaining parsley, then add to a small bowl with the chopped garlic.

9 Once the beef is tender, transfer the Dutch oven to the stove top. Using a slotted spoon, remove the bay leaves, herb bundles, onions, carrots, and crushed garlic cloves, then discard. Season the braising liquid to taste with salt and pepper. To the Dutch oven, add the bacon and the sautéed shallots, carrots, and mushrooms. Cook over low heat for 2 to 3 minutes, until the vegetables are warm.

10 Just before serving, stir the chopped garlic and parsley into the beef bourguignon. Serve with crusty bread or over buttered egg noodles. Or both!

THE GREAT BRITISH BAKING SHOW

Christmas Fruitcake

In the first episode of *The Great British Baking Show*'s seventh season, the bakers' signature bake is a fruitcake. Twenty-four-year-old sportswear designer Amelia impresses the judges with her family's Christmas fruitcake, a swirled Bundt with a homemade apricot glaze and marzipan stars. Amelia's swirled Bundt pan is called a Heritage Bundt pan, but any 6-cup Bundt pan will work here.

In our recipe, we bumped up the dried apricots in the classic cake, then added dried cranberries and a splash of pure vanilla extract as well. Amelia makes her marzipan on the stove top, but we've found that this food processor version is equally delicious and a little faster, too. Once your own fruitcake is baked, cut a thick slice, make yourself a cup of hot tea, and see what Paul and Prue have up their sleeves for the next group of hopeful bakers!

YIELD: 1 Bundt cake
PREP TIME: 25 minutes
COOK TIME: 2 hours, 30 minutes, plus cooling time

 **VEGETARIAN**

WATCH
THE GREAT BRITISH BAKING SHOW

CAKE

Nonstick baking spray for greasing

1¾ cups flour, plus more for dusting

1 cup almond flour

1 teaspoon kosher salt

1 cup dried apricots, finely chopped

¼ cup candied lemon peel, finely chopped

¼ cup candied orange peel, finely chopped

1 cup currants

1 cup golden raisins

½ cup dried cranberries

⅔ cup glacé cherries

⅓ cup plus 3 tablespoons orange brandy or liqueur, divided

1 cup plus 1 tablespoon unsalted butter, softened

1 medium orange

1 cup confectioners' sugar

½ cup light brown sugar, lightly packed

5 large eggs

2 teaspoons pure vanilla extract

MARZIPAN STARS

2 cups almond flour

1½ cups confectioners' sugar, plus more for dusting

Pinch of kosher salt

½ teaspoon pure vanilla extract

½ teaspoon orange brandy or liqueur

2 to 3 tablespoons water

GLAZE

One 8-ounce can apricots in juice, drained

⅔ cup granulated sugar

3 tablespoons orange brandy or liqueur, divided

2 teaspoons freshly squeezed lemon juice

1   **To make the cake:** Preheat the oven to 325°F/163°C with a rack in the center position. Generously coat a 6-cup Heritage Bundt pan with nonstick baking spray, then dust with flour, tapping out the excess. In a medium bowl, add the remaining 1¾ cups flour, almond flour, and salt, whisking to combine.

2   In a medium saucepan, combine the apricots, candied peels, currants, raisins, cranberries, glacé cherries, and ⅓ cup of the brandy or liqueur. Cover the saucepan, then simmer over low heat for about 5 minutes, until the dried fruit has softened and absorbed the alcohol. Transfer the fruits and any remaining liquid to a shallow bowl and let cool for about 15 minutes to room temperature. Wipe out the saucepan and reserve it for step 8.

3   Cut the softened butter into 1-tablespoon pieces. Finely grate the zest of 1 orange, then reserve ½ teaspoon for step 6. In the bowl of a stand mixer fitted with a paddle attachment, combine the butter, confectioners' sugar, light brown sugar, and the remaining orange zest. Beat on medium speed for about 5 minutes, until light and fluffy. Add the eggs, one at a time, beating well after each addition. Beat in the vanilla.

4   On low speed, add the dry ingredients, one-third at a time, until just combined. Fold in the cooled fruit. Scrape the batter into the prepared pan, then smooth the top with a rubber spatula.

5   Transfer the cake to the oven, then bake for 1 hour to 1 hour and 15 minutes, until a skewer inserted into the center comes out clean. Remove the pan to a wire cooling rack, then spoon the remaining 3 tablespoons of brandy over the top. Let the cake cool for 10 minutes, then invert it onto the wire rack. Cool completely.

6   **To make the marzipan stars:** Add the almond flour, 1½ cups of the confectioners' sugar, and the salt to the bowl of a food processor. Pulse to combine. Add the vanilla, brandy or liqueur, and reserved orange zest. Pulse once to combine. With the food processor running, add the water, 1 tablespoon at a time, until the marzipan begins to form a ball.

7   On a work surface lightly dusted with confectioners' sugar, knead the marzipan a few times to make a smooth ball with no dry spots. Roll the marzipan out to ¼-inch thickness, then use a 1-inch star cookie cutter to cut out 20 stars. (Reserve any extra marzipan for your own use.)

8   **To make the glaze:** In the reserved saucepan, combine the apricots and the sugar. Cook the mixture over low heat for about 5 minutes, until the sugar dissolves. Stir in 1 tablespoon of the brandy or liqueur. Increase the heat to medium, then cook, mashing the apricots with a spoon, for about 10 minutes, until the fruit is very soft and the mixture is jammy. Remove from the heat.

9   Set a fine-mesh strainer over a small bowl. Press the apricot glaze through the strainer, pushing on the solids with a spoon to extract all of the liquid. Discard the solids. Stir the lemon juice and the remaining 2 tablespoons of brandy into the glaze.

10   **To decorate the cake:** Brush a little of the glaze on the back of each marzipan star, then press onto the sides of the cake. Brush the remaining glaze over the cake and stars.

▶▶ Fast forward

No time to make the apricot mixture? Sub in warmed apricot preserves.

▶▶ **Fast forward**

Microwave the popcorn instead! Transfer the popcorn to a paper lunch bag. Roll down the top inch of the bag to seal. Microwave on high for 2 to 3 minutes, until the popcorn nearly stops popping. Let the bag stand closed for 1 minute, then transfer to the prepared bowl along with the pecans.

THE CHRISTMAS CHRONICLES 2

Explosive Gingerbread Popcorn

In *The Christmas Chronicles 2*, Mrs. Claus gives Jack some magical gingerbread cookies when he goes out in search of the levande root she needs to reverse the curse that Belsnickel put on the elves. Jack uses one to scare off Jola, Belsnickel's yule cat, when the big cat tries to attack him.

Mrs. Claus doesn't just make exploding cookies, though. She also makes healthy foods that "look and taste like foods you love." Hence, broccoli is a layer cake with bright green layers and lots of creamy frosting. Our festive gingerbread popcorn may not actually scare your enemies or be cauliflower in disguise, but there is a little health hidden in the spiced apple cider caramel, crunchy apple chips, and toasted pecans. It's the perfect snack to fuel all of your Netflix holiday movie marathons.

YIELD: 11 cups   **PREP TIME:** 30 minutes   **COOK TIME:** 1 hour

 VEGETARIAN   **GLUTEN FREE**

Nonstick baking spray for greasing

½ teaspoon vegetable oil

⅓ cup popcorn kernels

1½ teaspoons kosher salt, divided

⅔ cup pecan halves, coarsely chopped

1 orange

½-inch piece fresh ginger, thinly sliced

2 cinnamon sticks

1 cup apple cider

1 cup light brown sugar

4 tablespoons unsalted butter

2½ tablespoons light corn syrup

1 teaspoon ground ginger

½ teaspoon ground cinnamon

Pinch of ground cloves

¼ teaspoon baking soda

1 cup dried apple chips

¼ cup candied ginger, finely chopped

1   Preheat the oven to 250°F/121°C with a rack in the center position. Line a rimmed baking sheet with a nonstick baking mat or parchment paper and coat with nonstick baking spray. Lightly grease a large mixing bowl with nonstick spray.

2   In a medium pot, place the oil over high heat. Add the popcorn to the pot, then cover. Once the corn starts popping, shake the pot constantly until the popping stops. Remove the pot from the heat, then use a slotted spoon or ladle to transfer the popped corn to the prepared bowl, leaving any unpopped kernels behind. Season the popcorn with 1¼ teaspoons of the salt, then stir in the pecans.

3   Finely grate the zest from the orange. In a medium saucepan, combine the fresh ginger, cinnamon sticks, and apple cider. Bring to a simmer over medium heat, then reduce the heat to medium-low and cook for 15 to 20 minutes, until the cider has reduced to ¼ cup. Using a slotted spoon, remove the ginger slices and cinnamon sticks.

4   To the same saucepan, add the orange zest, brown sugar, butter, corn syrup, ground ginger, ground cinnamon, cloves, and the remaining ¼ teaspoon of salt. Increase the heat to medium, then cook for 10 to 12 minutes, until the caramel reaches 250°F/121°C on a candy thermometer. Add the baking soda, then remove the pan from the heat and stir to combine.

5   Working quickly, pour the caramel over the popcorn, then stir quickly to coat the popcorn in the caramel. Scrape onto the prepared baking sheet and pat into an even layer.

6   Transfer to the oven. Bake for 20 minutes, stirring halfway through, until the pecans are toasted. Remove from the oven. Stir in the apple chips and candied ginger. Let cool completely, then break into bite-sized chunks.

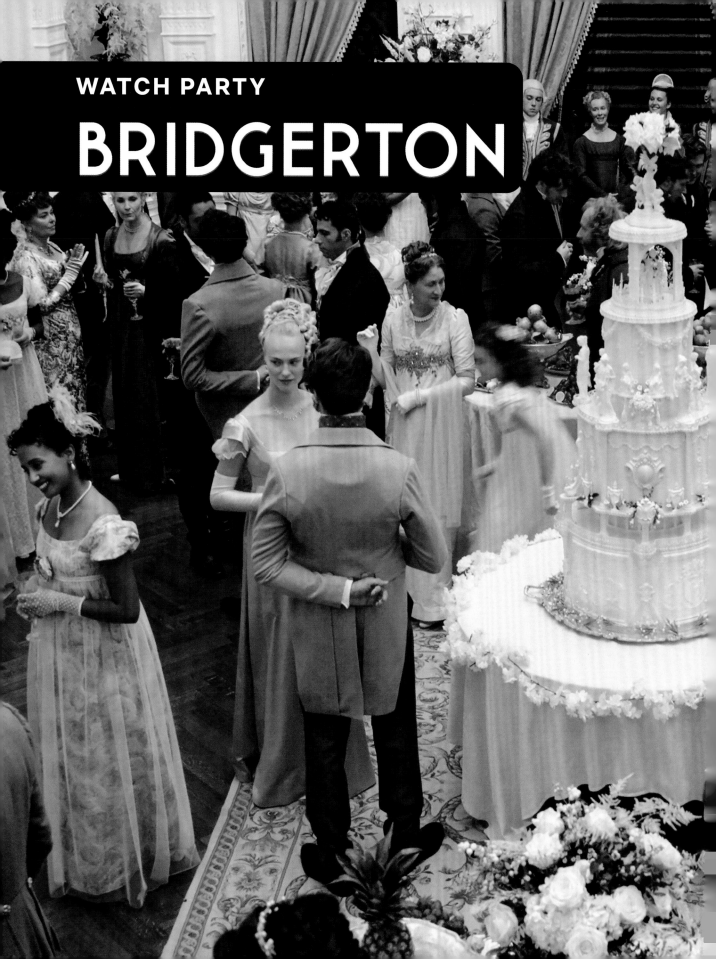

BRIDGERTON

Ready to watch—or rewatch—your favorite seasons of *Bridgerton*? Put your pinkies up, gather your friends, and throw an epic viewing party with these entertaining décor suggestions, activity ideas, recipes, and more!

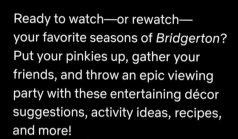

▶ **WATCH PARTY PLANNING**

WATCH PARTY PLANNING

If you think you're ready to take on the great social responsibility of hosting your very own *Bridgerton* watch party, then you haven't got a moment to spare. So, shine your silver, see the modiste, and check out these Watch Party ideas and suggestions.

▶ Setting the Scene

You'll be the talk of the town with these dashing displays.

- **Costume**: Have your guests come dressed in their best ball gown or Regency-era-inspired evening wear. Who doesn't want an excuse to dress up for a ball?

- **Craft**: Send your guests invitations via snail mail. Bonus points if they're handwritten using your best calligraphy.

- **Décor**: Bring out your finest silver and cutlery, line elegant platters with doilies to hold the delectable dishes you create, and light plenty of candles to set the mood.

▶ Pause & Play

- **Tabletop Croquet**: Take a break after each episode during your streaming sesh and stretch your legs with a game of tabletop croquet! Using wooden spoons as your mallets (or any other kitchen utensils that seem suitable), and a lemon as your croquet ball, clear off your table and have fun!

- **Let's Dance**: Either choreograph your own or learn a new group dance with your guests. (Psst: It doesn't have to be a Regency-era song either; perhaps one of today's top-ten hits.)

- **Sip-and-Paint**: Take a Sip-and-Paint approach to a traditional portrait, and have fun with it. After all, if it turns out awful it can always be "skied." (Note: "Skied" means to be hung higher up so it's harder to see, like when Benedict Bridgerton accidentally states in front of its creator that a painting should be "skied.")

- **Make Your Own Jewelry**: Get a selection of beads, chains, and other necklace supplies at your local craft store and set up a jewelry station for your guests. But don't use any rubies, otherwise you may be mistaken for Lord Featherington!

- **Identify the Song:** While streaming, have your guests identify the pop song that gets the instrumental treatment in the show. If you guess incorrectly, take a sip.

Cardamom Scones

During an impassioned conversation with Lady Danbury in the first episode of *Bridgerton*'s second season, Kate firmly declares "I despise English tea." Our scone recipe takes a classic English tea scone and spices it up with Indian flavors of cardamom, ginger, cinnamon, orange zest, and more. Because good scones require ample layers of clotted cream or butter and jam, we've also whipped up a fresh plum and ginger jam with Kate's favorite—a hint of cardamom.

YIELD: 8 scones
PREP TIME: 10 minutes
COOK TIME: 1 hour

 VEGETARIAN

PLUM & GINGER JAM

½ pound plums, halved, pitted, and cut into ½-inch pieces

¼-inch slice fresh ginger, peeled and finely chopped

½ cup granulated sugar

2 teaspoons freshly squeezed lemon juice

¼ teaspoon ground cardamom

SCONES

1 small orange

⅓ cup granulated sugar

2 cups all-purpose flour, plus more for dusting

2½ teaspoons baking powder

1¼ teaspoons ground cardamom

¾ teaspoon ground ginger

¾ teaspoon ground cinnamon

½ teaspoon kosher salt

⅛ teaspoon ground cloves

⅛ teaspoon ground coriander

½ cup cold unsalted butter

2 large eggs, divided

½ cup heavy cream

Turbinado sugar for sprinkling

Clotted cream or salted butter for serving

1 **To make the plum & ginger jam:** In a medium pot, combine the plums, ginger, and sugar. Cook over medium-high heat, stirring frequently, for about 10 minutes, until the plums are very soft and any juices have thickened.

2 To the same pot, add the lemon juice and cardamom, stirring to combine. Reduce the heat to medium, then continue cooking for about 5 minutes, until a spatula pulled through the jam will hold the gap for a few seconds before filling back in. Remove the jam from the heat and cool completely.

3 **To make the scones:** Finely grate the orange zest into a small bowl. Add the sugar to the same bowl, then rub the zest into the sugar until it is slightly damp and aromatic.

4 To a medium bowl, add 2 cups of the flour, the baking powder, cardamom, ginger, cinnamon, salt, cloves, and coriander, then whisk to combine. Whisk in the orange zest and sugar mixture.

5 Set a box grater in the flour mixture, then coarsely grate the cold butter on the side with the large holes. Lightly toss to coat the butter in the flour, then rub the butter into the flour with your hands or a pastry cutter until the mixture resembles coarse meal with a few larger butter pieces.

6 Make a well in the center of the butter and flour mixture, then crack 1 of the large eggs into the bowl. Add the heavy cream, then stir until just combined. Scrape onto a floured work surface, then gently knead the dough together.

7 Fold the dough in half, gently pressing the layers together. Rotate the dough one-quarter turn, then repeat the folding. Repeat the folding process two more times, then roll the dough out into a rectangle, about 1 inch thick.

8 Line a rimmed baking sheet with parchment paper. Using a 3-inch round cutter, cut the dough into scones, pressing the cutter straight down and lifting straight up. (Twisting the cutter will pinch the layers together and keep the scone from rising properly.) Transfer the scones to the prepared baking sheet as you go. Gently knead any scraps, then reroll the dough and cut out more scones. Let the scones rest at room temperature for 30 minutes.

9 Preheat the oven to 400°F/204°C with a rack in the center position. Crack the remaining egg into a bowl, then whisk to combine. Brush the tops of the scones with the egg, then sprinkle with turbinado sugar.

10 Transfer the scones to the oven, then bake for 10 to 12 minutes, until puffed and golden brown. Cool slightly, then serve with the plum jam and clotted cream or salted butter.

Shrimp Canapés

Whether you are dancing at a ball, strolling arm in arm on the promenade, or watching it all from your couch, these elegant puff pastry canapés stuffed with an herbed shrimp salad are the perfect bite.

YIELD: 16 canapés
PREP TIME: 20 minutes, plus thawing
COOK TIME: 50 minutes, plus chilling

PUFF PASTRY DIAMONDS

All-purpose flour for dusting

1 sheet store-bought puff pastry, defrosted in the refrigerator

1 large egg

POACHED SHRIMP SALAD

¾ cup white wine

2 bay leaves

2 sprigs fresh parsley

Kosher salt and freshly ground black pepper

1 lemon, halved

1 pound medium, peeled and deveined shrimp (size 41/50)

4 sprigs fresh tarragon

¼ cup mayonnaise

1 tablespoon olive oil

1 teaspoon Dijon mustard

½ teaspoon white wine vinegar

2 stalks celery, finely chopped

1 small bunch fresh chives (about ¼ ounce), finely chopped

1 **To make the puff pastry diamonds:** Line a rimmed baking sheet with parchment paper. On a lightly floured surface, roll one sheet of thawed puff pastry out into a 10-by-16-inch rectangle. Using a sharp knife, cut it into sixteen 2½-inch squares.

2 Working one at a time, turn the puff pastry square so it looks like a diamond. Fold the diamond in half, bottom point to top point. The shape now looks like a triangle. Starting with the left side, make one cut, ¼ inch from the edge, from the bottom corner to ¼ inch below the top. Repeat on the right side. Open the shape back into a diamond. Bring the left side across the diamond to the right, then cross the right side over to the left. You will now have a diamond shape with twisted points on the top and bottom and a raised border on the sides. Transfer to the prepared baking sheet and repeat with the remaining squares.

3 Crack the egg into a small bowl, then lightly beat with a fork. Brush the borders lightly with egg wash. (Do not brush the sides.) Transfer to the refrigerator and chill for 15 to 20 minutes, until the egg wash is set and the pastry has firmed up again.

4 Preheat the oven to 375°F/190°F with a rack in the center position. Place the pastry diamonds in the oven and bake, rotating the baking sheet halfway through, for 25 to 30 minutes, until puffed and golden. Transfer the diamonds to a wire cooling rack while you prepare the shrimp filling.

5 **To make the poached shrimp salad:** In a medium pot, combine 2 cups of cold water, the wine, bay leaves, parsley, 1 teaspoon of kosher salt, and a few grinds of fresh pepper. Squeeze the lemon halves into the same pot, then add the halves as well. Cover and bring to a boil. Reduce the heat to medium, then simmer for 5 minutes.

6 To the same pot, add half of the shrimp, then simmer for 1 to 2 minutes, until opaque. Using a slotted spoon, transfer the cooked shrimp to a plate to cool. Repeat with the remaining shrimp. Chop all of the cooked shrimp into ½-inch pieces. Put the shrimp in the refrigerator until cool, about 5 minutes.

7 Remove the tarragon leaves from the stems, then finely chop 1 teaspoon (save any remaining tarragon for your own use). In a medium bowl, combine the mayonnaise, olive oil, mustard, and vinegar, stirring until smooth. Season to taste with salt and pepper, then stir in the shrimp, celery, tarragon, and half of the chives.

8 Spoon the shrimp salad in the center of the puff pastry diamonds, then garnish with the remaining chives.

Ricotta and Honey Tea Sandwiches

As a *Bridgerton* fan, you've undoubtedly noticed bees appearing in the oddest places, including embroidered on Benedict's shirt. But this buzziness culminates when we learn that the late Viscount Edmund Bridgerton died after being stung by a bee after he picked a flower for his wife. We honor the sweetness of the family he left behind with these elegant tea sandwiches. Quick to make and delicious to eat, these bites are equally at home as part of a larger *Bridgerton* spread or as an easy snack before pressing "play" for the next episode.

YIELD: 12 tea sandwiches
PREP TIME: 20 minutes

1 lemon

1 cup fresh ricotta cheese

Kosher salt and freshly ground black pepper

8 slices very thin white sandwich bread

2 medium nectarines, halved, pitted, and thinly sliced

½ cup blackberries, halved

1 tablespoon honey

1 In a medium bowl, finely grate the zest of the lemon. To the same bowl, add the ricotta, then stir until smooth. Season to taste with salt and pepper.

2 Arrange the bread on a work surface, then divide the ricotta among the slices and spread it into an even layer. Arrange the nectarines in an even layer on two of the slices, then place the blackberries on two other slices. Drizzle the fruit with the honey, then top with the remaining slices of bread.

3 Using a sharp knife, cut the crusts off the bread, then cut each sandwich into three rectangles.

Tea Fit for a Lady

To quench your thirst as you wait for the next elegant shoe to drop, we offer a *Bridgerton*-worthy version of an Arnold Palmer. Here, the sweetness of the ginger-thyme lemonade reflects the opportunities for love and sweet gossip at every turn, and the bracing Earl Grey tea will provide just enough caffeine to keep you cheerful until Lady Whistledown's next missive appears.

YIELD: 4 servings
PREP TIME: 10 minutes
COOK TIME: 30 minutes, plus chilling

 VEGAN GLUTEN FREE

7 cups water, divided

1 cup granulated sugar

1 sprig lemon thyme, plus more for garnishing

⅛-inch piece fresh ginger, thinly sliced into matchsticks

¾ cup freshly squeezed lemon juice

1 orange

5 Earl Grey tea bags

Ice for serving

1 To a small saucepan, add 1 cup of the water, the sugar, 1 sprig of lemon thyme, and ginger.

2 Place the saucepan on the stove top, then heat over low, stirring, for about 3 minutes, until the sugar has dissolved. Increase the heat to medium, then bring the syrup to a simmer. Cook, stirring occasionally, for about 4 minutes, until the syrup is fragrant and has reduced slightly. Remove from the heat, then let cool for 10 minutes. Remove the thyme and ginger.

3 In a large liquid measuring cup, combine the syrup, 2 cups of water, and the lemon juice. Refrigerate the lemonade for about 30 minutes, until chilled.

4 Using a vegetable peeler, remove two 2-inch pieces of orange zest. In a medium pot, add the remaining 4 cups of water, then bring to a boil. Add the zest and tea bags, then remove from the heat. Let steep for 7 minutes, then discard the tea bags and zest. Refrigerate the tea for about 30 minutes, until chilled.

5 Divide the lemonade among four highball glasses, then fill the glasses halfway with ice. Top with the iced tea, then garnish with sprigs of lemon thyme.

WATCH
BRIDGERTON

So-Good-You'll-Lick-the-Spoon Mini Ice Cream Pies

Inspired by Gunter's and the popularity of ice cream among the elite in Regency England, we created these individual ice cream pies. For this recipe, ice cream flavored with lemon zest and candied ginger is spooned in buttery pâte sucrée tart shells and then topped with fresh apricots, apricot jam, and finely chopped pistachios. If you don't have mini tart pans, you can use one 8- or 9-inch tart pan with a removable bottom and make one larger tart.

YIELD: 4 mini ice cream pies
PREP TIME: 15 minutes
COOK TIME: 1 hour 15 minutes, plus 3 hours chilling

🌿 **VEGETARIAN**

1 cup plus 2 tablespoons all-purpose flour, plus more for dusting

¼ cup plus 1 teaspoon granulated sugar, divided

¼ teaspoon kosher salt

½ cup unsalted butter

1 egg yolk

2 tablespoons heavy cream

2 lemons

¼ cup candied ginger, finely chopped

3 cups vanilla ice cream, softened

1 teaspoon lemon liqueur (optional)

2 tablespoons apricot jam

5 fresh apricots, halved, pitted, and thinly sliced

3 tablespoons pistachios, finely chopped

>>recipe continues
on the next page

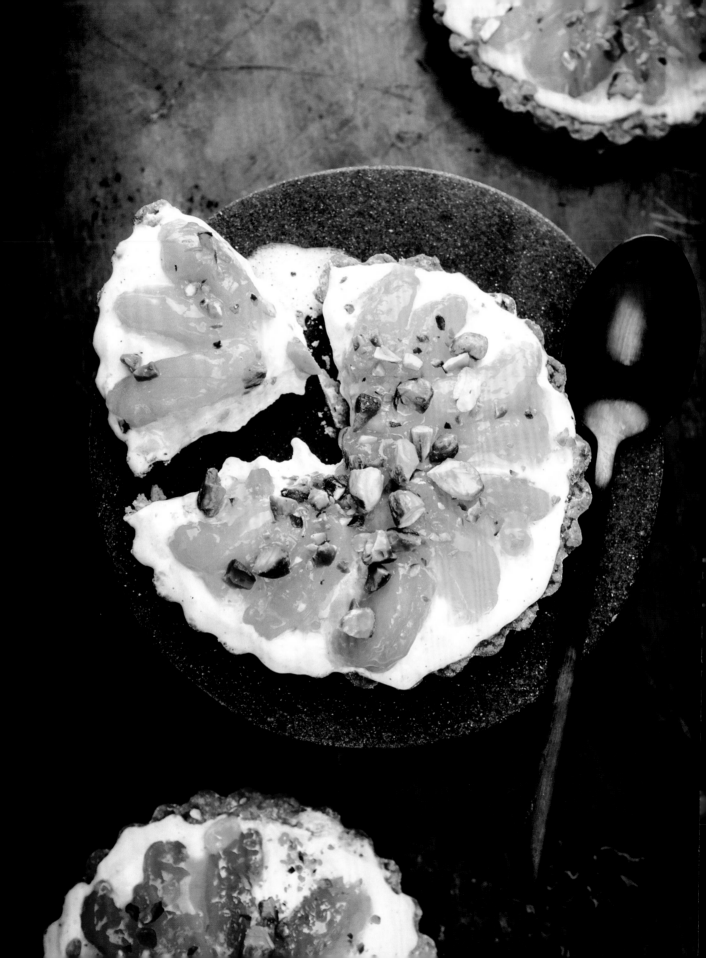

>>Mini Ice Cream Pies continued

1 **To make the tart dough:** In a large bowl, add the flour, ¼ cup of the sugar, and salt, whisking until combined. Cut the butter into small pieces, then add to the bowl with the flour. Using your hands, work the butter into the flour until the mixture looks like coarse bread crumbs. Make a well in the dry ingredients, then add the egg yolk and heavy cream. Whisk the yolk and cream with a fork until just combined. Use a spatula to stir the wet ingredients into the dry, until the dough comes together. Transfer the dough to a lightly floured surface. Knead a few times, then shape it into a disk about 1 inch thick. Cut the dough into quarters, then pat each piece into a smaller disk. Wrap each piece in plastic wrap, then refrigerate for about 1 hour, until firm.

2 On a lightly floured surface, roll each piece of dough into a 6-inch circle. Using your fingers, pat the dough across the bottom and up the sides of a 4-inch tart pan. Trim off any excess dough. Transfer to the refrigerator and chill while you repeat with the remaining three disks.

3 Preheat the oven to 350°F/177°C with a rack in the center of the oven. Place the tarts on a rimmed baking sheet. Line each tart pan with a 5-inch square of parchment paper and fill with pie weights or dried beans. Transfer to the oven, then bake for 15 to 20 minutes, until golden brown. Remove the parchment and pie weights, then return to the oven and bake for about 10 minutes, until the bottoms are lightly browned. Transfer to a wire rack and cool completely.

4 Carefully remove the tart shells from the pans. Transfer the tart shells to a rimmed baking sheet.

5 Finely grate the zest from the lemons. To a medium bowl, add the lemon zest, ginger, ice cream, and lemon liqueur, if desired, then stir to combine.

6 Divide the ice cream among the tart shells, then use a spatula to smooth the tops. Transfer to the freezer, then chill for at least 3 hours, until very firm.

7 Just before serving, add the apricot jam and 1 teaspoon of water to a small microwave-safe bowl. Microwave on high for about 15 seconds, until the jam is slightly loosened. In a small bowl, add the apricots and remaining 1 teaspoon of sugar, then stir to combine.

8 Arrange the apricot slices in overlapping concentric circles on top of the ice cream, then brush the fruit with the jam. Sprinkle with the pistachios and serve immediately.

153

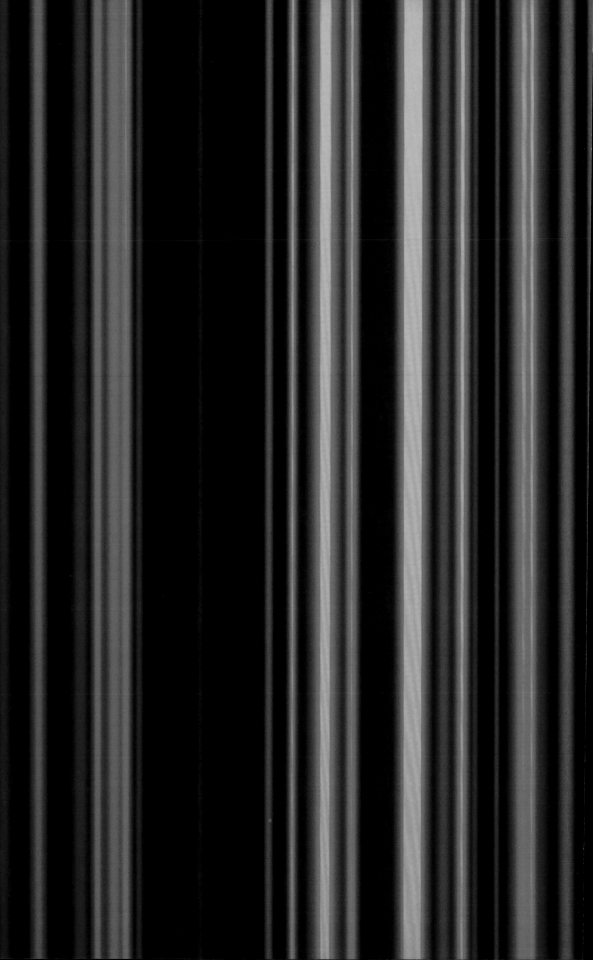

Sweet Inspirations

Like the perfect ending to any meal, this desserts chapter is chockful of sugary goodness gleaned from some of Netflix's sweetest shows and inspired by other memorable films and series.

COCONUT–GRAHAM CRACKER CAKE

¾ cup unsalted butter

Nonstick baking spray for greasing

18 graham crackers (about 9¾ ounces)

¾ cup sweetened flaked coconut

¾ cup all-purpose flour

3¼ teaspoons baking powder

¾ teaspoon salt

1 cup granulated sugar

3 large eggs

1½ teaspoons pure vanilla extract

1½ teaspoons coconut rum (optional)

1 cup plus 2 tablespoons whole milk

SALTED CARAMEL FILLING

½ cup granulated sugar

1 tablespoon light corn syrup

2 tablespoons water

½ cup heavy cream

2 tablespoons sour cream

¾ teaspoon kosher salt

COCONUT BUTTERCREAM

¾ cup unsalted butter

5 cups confectioners' sugar, divided

1 teaspoon pure vanilla extract

½ teaspoon kosher salt

¾ cup canned unsweetened coconut milk

Blue food coloring

Mermaid or under-the-sea sprinkles (optional)

SUGAR RUSH

Sweet & Salty Oceanic Ombre Cake

On the "Cake by the Ocean" episode of *Sugar Rush*, the final two teams are tasked by guest judge Richard Blais with creating cakes that show an underwater seascape. The winning team, Rebecca and Jenn, create a whimsical bakery scene on top of their chocolate and coffee buttercream cake, complete with an octopus in a chef hat.

Inspired by these aquatic confections, we built our own sea-inspired cake. Coconut-graham cake layers remind us of warm, sandy beaches, while ombre coconut buttercream evokes the deeper blues of the ocean itself.

YIELD: One 8-inch cake   **PREP TIME:** 35 minutes, plus softening
COOK TIME: 1 hour 30 minutes, plus cooling

 VEGETARIAN

1 **To make the coconut–graham cracker cakes:** Place the butter on the counter for about 40 minutes to soften. Preheat the oven to 350°F/177°C with a rack in the center position. Coat three 8-inch cake pans with nonstick baking spray, then line the bottom of the pans with parchment paper. In a food processor, pulse the graham crackers until fine crumbs form. (You should have 2¼ cups of crumbs.)

2 Place the coconut on a pie plate, then spread it into an even layer. Toast the coconut in the oven for 5 to 7 minutes, until browned. Remove from the oven, then cool completely.

3 To a medium bowl, add the graham cracker crumbs, flour, baking powder, and salt, then whisk to combine.

4 Cut the softened butter into 1-inch chunks, then transfer to the bowl of a stand mixer fitted with a paddle attachment. Add the sugar to the same bowl. On medium speed, beat the butter and sugar for 3 to 5 minutes, until light and fluffy. Add the eggs, one at a time, beating well after each addition. Add the vanilla and coconut rum, if desired. On low speed, mix in one-third of the dry ingredients, then add about half of the milk and mix until just combined. Repeat with the remaining dry ingredients and milk, ending with the last third of the dry ingredients. Sprinkle the toasted coconut over the top, then fold in to combine.

>>recipe continues on the next page

5 Divide the cake batter among the cake pans, then smooth the tops with a spatula. Bake on the center rack for 20 to 25 minutes, until the cake springs back lightly to the touch and a toothpick inserted into the center comes out clean.

6 Transfer to wire cooling racks and cool for 10 minutes. Invert each cake onto a second wire rack, remove the parchment paper, and then carefully flip it back over so the domed top side is up. Cool completely.

7 **To make the salted caramel:** In a medium saucepan, combine the sugar, corn syrup, and water, then very carefully stir so the sugar is evenly moistened (avoid splashing any sugar up on the sides). Cook over high heat for about 5 minutes, until the sugar mixture reaches 350°F/177°C on an instant-read thermometer and is a dark amber color. Remove the saucepan from the heat. Carefully whisk in the heavy cream and the salt, then whisk in the sour cream (the mixture will bubble up). Transfer to a medium bowl and cool to room temperature.

8 **To make the coconut buttercream:** Place the butter on the counter for about 40 minutes to come to room temperature. Sift 4½ cups of the confectioners' sugar into a bowl to remove any lumps. Cut the butter into ½-inch pieces, then transfer to the bowl of a stand mixer fitted with a paddle attachment. Beat the butter on medium speed for 2 to 3 minutes, until light and fluffy. On low speed, beat in the confectioners' sugar, vanilla, salt, and coconut milk until combined. Increase the speed to medium, then beat for 2 to 3 minutes, until light and fluffy. If the frosting seems too soft, add additional confectioners' sugar, ¼ cup at a time.

9 **To assemble the cake:** Using a serrated knife, trim off the domed tops of the cake layers. Transfer one cake layer, cut side up, to a cake stand or platter. Place ⅔ cup of the coconut buttercream on top of the cake, then spread into an even layer. Spread half of the salted caramel on top of the buttercream, leaving a ½-inch border. Top with the second cake layer. Spread another ⅔ cup of the buttercream on the top of the cake and top with the remaining caramel. Place the last cake layer on top, then spread ⅔ cup of the buttercream on top. Coat the sides of the cake with a thin layer of buttercream, then transfer to the refrigerator for about 30 minutes, until the frosting is firm.

10 Divide the remaining frosting among five bowls. Color the frosting in four of the bowls with blue food coloring, increasing the amount for each bowl so the colors get darker as you go, creating the ombre effect. Scrape the white frosting into a piping bag fitted with a round tip. Pipe a ring of white frosting around the top of the cake. Squeeze any remaining white frosting back into its original bowl, then fill the piping bag with the lightest shade of blue. Pipe a ring of the light blue under the ring of white, then repeat the process, from lightest to darkest, with the remaining frosting.

11 Using a bench scraper or cake smoother and slowly turning the cake stand or platter, hold the straight side against the cake and slowly remove the excess frosting from the side of the cake. With a knife, sweep the icing up to resemble the ocean waves.

To All the Boys
ALWAYS AND FOREVER

Hidden Heart Cupcakes

CUPCAKES

½ cup unsalted butter

Nonstick cooking spray

2 cups all-purpose flour

1 tablespoon baking powder

¾ teaspoon kosher salt

1½ cups granulated sugar

1 lemon

3 large eggs

1 cup whole milk

⅛ teaspoon red food coloring

½ teaspoon raspberry liqueur or extract (optional)

1 teaspoon pure vanilla extract

TWO-TONE BUTTERCREAM

½ cup unsalted butter

1 lemon

Pinch of kosher salt

4 cups confectioners' sugar, divided

⅓ cup heavy cream

Yellow food coloring

¼ teaspoon raspberry liqueur or extract (optional)

Red food coloring

Multicolored or heart sprinkles for decorating (optional)

Based on the novel *Always and Forever, Lara Jean* by Jenny Han, *To All the Boys: Always and Forever* continues the love story of Lara Jean Covey and Peter Kavinsky as they approach their senior year of high school. When the movie begins, Lara Jean is writing Peter a letter from the 2D Greem Cafe in Seoul, South Korea. While Lara Jean talks about Peter, she enjoys cupcakes with swoops of neon-hued frosting.

Just like Lara Jean's love was first written down in letters and hidden in a box, the surprise in this two-toned lemon cupcake is hidden in the cake. A piping bag and tip will help you achieve the swirled frosting shown in the scene from the 2D Greem Cafe, and over-the-top sprinkles, while definitely optional, evoke Lara Jean's brightly colored, flowery bedroom.

YIELD: 12 cupcakes
PREP TIME: 1 hour, plus 1 hour 30 minutes cooling
COOK TIME: 30 minutes

🌿 **VEGETARIAN**

1 **To make the cupcakes:** Place the butter on the counter for about 40 minutes to soften to room temperature. Line a 12-cup cupcake tin with paper liners. Grease an 8-inch baking dish with nonstick spray, then line with parchment paper, extending it up two sides. Preheat the oven to 350°F/177°C with a rack in the center position.

2 To a small bowl, add the flour, baking powder, and kosher salt, whisking to combine. Cut the softened butter into 1-inch pieces, then add it to a medium bowl along with the granulated sugar. Finely grate the zest of the lemon, then place it in the same bowl. Using a hand mixer on medium speed, beat the butter, sugar, and lemon zest for 2 to 3 minutes, until light and fluffy. On medium-low speed, add the eggs one at a time, scraping down the bowl as needed. On low speed, alternate adding the flour mixture and milk, beginning and ending with the flour mixture. Mix until just combined.

3 Place 1½ cups of the cupcake batter in a medium bowl, then stir in the red food coloring. Add the raspberry liqueur or extract, if desired. (Add more red food coloring, a drop or two at a time, if you want the batter to be a darker red.) Scrape the batter into the prepared baking pan, then smooth the surface with a spatula. Transfer to the center rack of the oven and bake for about 12 minutes, until a toothpick inserted into the center of the cake comes out clean. Remove to a wire rack and cool completely.

>>recipe continues on the next page

>>Hidden Heart Cupcakes continued

4 Using the parchment overhang, carefully lift the red cake out of the baking pan and transfer to a cutting board. Cut out 12 heart shapes with a 1-inch cookie cutter. (Snack on any scraps!)

5 Stir the vanilla extract into the remaining batter. Divide half of the batter among each lined cup in the cupcake tin. Carefully place one heart vertically in the center of each cup, then top with the remaining batter.

6 Transfer the tin to the oven and bake for 16 to 18 minutes, until the cupcakes are set and a toothpick inserted into the center comes out clean. Cool completely.

7 **To make the two-toned buttercream:** While the cupcakes are baking, let the butter soften at room temperature for about 40 minutes. Cut the softened butter into ½-inch pieces, then place in a medium bowl. Finely grate the zest of the lemon, then add it to the butter. Using a hand mixer, beat the butter mixture on medium speed for 3 to 4 minutes, until smooth and creamy. Add the salt and ½ cup of the confectioners' sugar, then beat on low speed until the sugar is incorporated. Add the remaining confectioners' sugar, ½ cup at a time, then add the heavy cream. Beat on medium speed for 2 to 3 minutes, until light and fluffy.

8 Transfer half of the buttercream to a second bowl. Stir in the yellow food coloring, one or two drops at a time, until the buttercream is a sunny yellow. To the remaining buttercream, stir in the raspberry liqueur or extract, if desired, then add the red food coloring, a drop or two at a time, until the frosting is a bright pink.

9 **To decorate the cupcakes:** Fit a piping bag with a star or round tip, then fold down the top of the piping bag. Carefully spread the yellow buttercream down one side of the bag all the way to the tip, then add the pink buttercream to the other side. Unroll the top of the bag, then twist the top of the bag together. Pipe swirls of the tone-toned buttercream on top of the cooled cupcakes, then garnish with sprinkles, if desired. Share with someone you love!

THE
QUEEN'S GAMBIT
Chocolate Chessboard Cake

While Beth is still in the orphanage at the beginning of *The Queen's Gambit*, she lies in bed, imagining a chessboard on the ceiling and going through ever-more-complicated plays in her mind.

Now, we might not drift to sleep imagining chess plays, but imagining a chessboard-inspired cake? That is truly a sweet dream! Like the classic English Battenberg cake, this Chocolate Chessboard Cake uses two flavors of cake, here vanilla and chocolate, to create the distinct checked pattern. The decadent creation is the perfect fuel to watch Beth Harmon perfect her own use of the Queen's Gambit.

YIELD: One 7-inch cake **PREP TIME:** 20 minutes **COOK TIME:** 45 minutes, plus chilling

 VEGETARIAN

12 ounces bittersweet chocolate, coarsely chopped

1 cup heavy cream

1 teaspoon salt

¾ cup unsalted butter, at room temperature

One 11-ounce vanilla pound cake

One 11-ounce chocolate pound cake

Confectioners' sugar and unsweetened cocoa powder for decorating

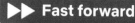 **Fast forward**

To create the stencil designs: Using a piece of thin cardboard, draw the outline of a Queen chess piece that is about 1 inch tall. Using a razor or exacto knife, cut out the inside of the stencil and discard. Place the stencil on one section of the cake top, then sift a layer of powdered sugar to fill in shape. Repeat a few more times. Then, sift unsweetened cocoa powder over the stencil a few times.

1 **To make the whipped ganache frosting:** Add the bittersweet chocolate to a medium heatproof bowl. In a small saucepan, heat the heavy cream over medium-high for 1 to 2 minutes, until it begins to steam. Pour the hot cream over the chocolate in the bowl and let stand for about 5 minutes, until the chocolate begins to melt. (Alternatively, heat the cream in a medium microwave-safe bowl for 45 seconds to 1 minute, until just steaming. Add the chocolate to the bowl, then let stand for 5 minutes and proceed with the recipe.) Add the salt and whisk until smooth. Let the ganache stand at room temperature, stirring occasionally, for about 40 minutes, until cooled to room temperature (around 75°F/24°C).

2 Transfer the cooled ganache to the bowl of a stand mixer fitted with a paddle attachment. Beat the ganache on low, adding the butter 1 tablespoon at a time, and fully incorporating it before adding the next piece. Once all of the butter has been incorporated, beat on medium speed for about 3 minutes, until the whipped ganache frosting is light and fluffy.

3 Trim the domed top off each pound cake, then cut each cake into two even layers (each about 1 inch thick).

4 **To build the chessboard cake layers:** Place one vanilla pound cake layer on a cutting board, then spread the top with ¼ cup of the whipped ganache. Place a chocolate layer on top of the ganache, then spread the top with another ¼ cup of the ganache in an even layer. Repeat with the remaining vanilla and chocolate pound cake layers. Transfer to the refrigerator and chill for 10 minutes, until the layers are firm.

5 Carefully cut the stacked cake lengthwise into three even layers (each about 1 inch wide). Place one layer, cut side up, on a serving platter or cake stand. Spread the layer with ¼ cup of whipped ganache. Place another layer on top, making sure that the stripes of chocolate cake are over the vanilla pound cake and vice versa. Spread with ¼ cup of the whipped ganache. Repeat with the remaining cake layer, again alternating chocolate over vanilla, and another ¼ cup of ganache. Trim a thin slice from the short ends of the cake to create flat sides. Spread a thin layer of ganache over the top and sides of the cake. (This is called the crumb layer and will trap any loose cake crumbs.) Refrigerate for about 30 minutes, until the ganache is firm. Spread remaining whipped ganache over top and sides of the cake.

BIRD BOX

Mixed-Berry Hand Pies

In the postapocalyptic movie *Bird Box*, a small group of survivors hide from unseen forces that are wreaking havoc on the human race. If a person even looks at the creatures stalking them, it will kill them. To find supplies, the remaining people must carefully make their way to abandoned homes or stores while they are blindfolded.

On one such supply run, Malorie finds a box of strawberry toaster pastries in the kitchen of an abandoned home. She shares the treat with fellow survivor Tom and two young children who are simply called Boy and Girl. As they eat, the stale pastry reminds the two adults of happier times and offers a moment of simple sweetness for the kids.

YIELD: 8 hand pies
PREP TIME: 50 minutes, plus chilling
COOK TIME: 40 minutes

 VEGETARIAN

WATCH
BIRD BOX

PIE DOUGH

2½ cups all-purpose flour, plus more for dusting

3½ teaspoons granulated sugar

1 teaspoon kosher salt

1 cup cold unsalted butter

½ cup ice water

BERRY FILLING

5 medium strawberries, hulled and coarsely chopped

⅔ cup blueberries

⅔ cup raspberries

1 lemon

¼ teaspoon kosher salt

½ cup granulated sugar

2 tablespoons cornstarch

1 large egg

1 tablespoon water

FROSTING

1 cup confectioners' sugar

1 to 2 tablespoons milk

¼ teaspoon pure vanilla extract

Pinch of kosher salt

Purple food coloring or red, yellow, and green food colorings

Sprinkles for decorating (optional)

1 **To make the pie dough:** In the bowl of a food processor, add the flour, sugar, and salt, then pulse to combine. Cut the butter into ½-inch pieces, then transfer to the food processor. Pulse until the butter is in pea-sized pieces. Drizzle in ¼ cup of the water, then pulse until a shaggy dough forms. (Add more water, 1 tablespoon at a time, as needed, if the dough is too dry.)

2 Transfer the dough to a lightly floured surface, then knead a few times until a smooth dough forms. Divide the dough in half, then pat each portion into a rectangle about 1 inch thick. Wrap in plastic wrap, then refrigerate for about 1 hour, until firm.

3 **To make the berry filling:** In a small saucepan, combine the strawberries, blueberries, and raspberries. Finely grate the zest of the lemon, then add the zest to the same saucepan. Halve the lemon, then squeeze the juice from one half into saucepan (save the other half for your own use). Sprinkle the berries with salt.

4 Cover the saucepan, then cook over low heat for 5 to 7 minutes, until the berries are soft and beginning to break down. Meanwhile, in a small bowl, whisk the sugar and the cornstarch to combine. Once the berries are soft, coarsely mash them with a spoon or potato masher. Stir in the sugar-cornstarch mixture, then continue cooking over low, stirring frequently, for 2 to 3 minutes, until the sugar has dissolved and the filling has thickened. Remove from the heat and cool completely.

5 **To assemble the hand pies:** In a small bowl, crack the egg, then beat it with the water until the yolk and white are combined. Line a rimmed baking sheet with parchment paper.

6 On a lightly floured surface, roll one piece of dough out to ⅛ inch thick, then trim to make a 9-by-12-inch rectangle. With the long side facing you, cut the dough into 3-inch-wide strips. Brush the strips with the egg wash.

7 On the bottom half of each strip, add 1½ tablespoons of the berry filling. Spread the filling into a 3-inch rectangle, leaving a ½-inch border. Fold the top half of the dough over the filling, then use your fingers to seal the hand pie on all sides. Use the tines of a fork to create a decorative seal around all four sides. Carefully transfer the hand pies to the prepared baking sheet, 1-inch apart, then repeat with the remaining pie dough and jam. (You may have some jam left over.) Transfer the hand pies to the refrigerator, then chill for 10 to 15 minutes, until the dough is firm.

8 Preheat the oven to 350°F/177°C with a rack in the center position. Brush the tops of the hand pies with the remaining egg wash. Transfer to the oven, then bake the pies for 25 to 30 minutes, until deeply browned. Cool the pies on the baking sheet for 10 minutes, then place on a wire rack to cool completely.

9 **To finish the hand pies:** In a medium bowl, combine the confectioners' sugar, 1 tablespoon of the milk, vanilla, and salt, then whisk until smooth. Add the remaining milk, 1 teaspoon at a time, until the frosting is thick enough to coat the top of the pies without running over the sides. To tint the frosting purple, use either purple food coloring or a drop or two each of red, yellow, and green until the desired color is achieved.

10 Spoon the frosting on the cooled hand pies, then decorate with the sprinkles, if desired.

 Fast forward

Want to get these delicious treats on the table faster? Here are a couple of handy shortcuts:

1. Need to skip the homemade pie dough and start the movie? You can use three premade piecrust rounds instead of the homemade version.

2. Don't want to make the berry filling? In a small saucepan, combine 1 tablespoon cornstarch and 1 teaspoon water, then stir to combine. To the same saucepan, add ¾ cup fruit preserves and the juice of half a lemon. Over medium heat, bring the jam mixture to a boil, then cook for 2 to 3 minutes, until thickened slightly. Cool completely.

JUNIOR BAKING SHOW

Technicolor Cookies

On the *Junior Baking Show*, hosts Liam Charles and Ravneet Gill cheer and gently coach the young bakers through two challenges on each episode. Working under time constraints that would make even the most seasoned adult baker sweat, the *Junior* contestants whip up tender cakes, whimsical biscuits, and more.

During the second episode of the sixth season, the bakers have to make a fantasy, storybook scene out of decorated biscuits. Our confetti sugar cookies, with their colorful candy centers, would have been right at home in this challenge, the perfect colorful cookie to complete any storybook scene.

YIELD: 24 cookies
PREP TIME: 15 minutes
COOK TIME:
1 hour 15 minutes,
plus 3 hours chilling

 VEGETARIAN

1 cup unsalted butter

1⅓ cups hard candies, preferably in 3 to 4 different colors

3 cups all-purpose flour

¾ teaspoon baking powder

½ teaspoon kosher salt

1 medium orange

1 lemon

1¼ cups granulated sugar

4 large egg yolks

1 teaspoon pure vanilla extract

¾ cup rainbow sprinkles

1 Place the butter on the counter for about 40 minutes to soften. Add each color of candy to a separate resealable quart-sized plastic bag, then use a rolling pin to crush the candy. To a medium bowl, add the flour, baking powder, and salt, then whisk to combine.

2 Finely grate the zest from the orange and lemon. In a large bowl or the bowl of a stand mixer fitted with a paddle attachment, combine the butter, sugar, and orange and lemon zests. Beat on medium speed for 3 to 4 minutes, until light and fluffy. Add the egg yolks, one at a time, mixing well after each addition, then add the vanilla.

3 On low speed, mix in the dry ingredients and the sprinkles until just combined. Divide the dough in half, then pat each portion into a square about 1 inch thick. Wrap in plastic wrap, then chill for about 1 hour, until firm.

4 Working with one piece of dough at a time, roll the dough out between two pieces of parchment paper to ⅛-inch thickness. Put the dough back in the refrigerator, then chill for 20 to 30 minutes, until firm. Repeat with the second piece of dough.

5 Preheat the oven to 350°F/177°C with a rack in the center position. Line a rimmed baking sheet with parchment paper. Using a 3-inch cookie cutter, cut the dough into shapes. Place the cut-out cookies on the prepared baking sheet, then use a 1-inch cookie cutter to remove the center of the shape. Gather up any cookie dough scraps, pat into a square, wrap in plastic, and chill before rerolling.

6 Transfer the cookies to the oven and bake for 8 to 10 minutes, until just set. Sprinkle about 1 teaspoon of crushed candy into the center of each cookie. Return to the oven, then bake for 2 to 3 minutes more, until the candy has melted and the cookie edges are lightly browned. Remove from the oven. Let the cookies cool on the baking sheet for 10 minutes, then transfer to a wire rack to cool completely. Repeat with remaining cookie dough and candy.

FLOOR IS LAVA

Oozing Lava Cakes

On *Floor Is Lava*, three teams leap across a wild-and-wacky obstacle course, trying to reach the exit. The catch? The floor is lava (well, a vicious red goop that looks a whole lot like lava). If you fall in, you're out of the game.

    While you watch and root for your favorite team, dig into an entirely more delicious kind of lava. Espresso powder, good quality bittersweet chocolate, and a splash of hazelnut liqueur give these warm chocolate cakes a particularly elegant flavor. You can also add coffee or raspberry liqueur in place of the hazelnut, or omit it entirely.

YIELD: 4 cakes **PREP TIME:** 25 minutes **COOK TIME:** 10 minutes

 VEGETARIAN

½ cup unsalted butter, plus more for greasing

2 tablespoons unsweetened cocoa powder plus more for dusting, divided

6 ounces bittersweet chocolate, finely chopped

½ teaspoon espresso powder

1 teaspoon pure vanilla extract

1 teaspoon hazelnut liqueur (optional)

2 large eggs

2 large egg yolks

¼ cup granulated sugar

Pinch of kosher salt

Ice cream, confectioners' sugar, or berries for serving (optional)

1 Preheat the oven to 450°F/232°C with a rack in the center position. Lightly butter four 6-ounce ramekins, then dust with cocoa powder and tap out the excess. Transfer the prepared ramekins to a baking sheet.

2 Cut the butter into small pieces. Fill a medium pot halfway with water, then bring to a simmer. In a medium metal bowl, combine the chocolate, butter, and espresso powder. Place the bowl over the simmering water (the bottom of the bowl should not touch the water), then cook, stirring occasionally, until the butter and nearly all of the chocolate have melted, 7 to 10 minutes. Remove the bowl from the heat, add the vanilla and liqueur, if desired, then stir until the mixture is smooth. (Alternatively, add the chocolate, butter, and espresso powder to a large bowl. Microwave on 50% power in 30-second increments until the chocolate is nearly melted. Remove from the microwave, then stir until the chocolate mixture is smooth.)

3 While the chocolate melts, combine the eggs, egg yolks, sugar, and salt in a large bowl or the bowl of a stand mixer fitted with the whisk attachment. Whip on high speed for about 3 minutes, until pale and thick.

4 Sprinkle the 2 tablespoons of cocoa powder over the beaten eggs, then add the warm chocolate, one-third at a time, folding to combine. (Don't overmix!)

5 Divide the chocolate batter among the ramekins. Transfer to the oven, then bake for 8 to 10 minutes, until the tops are set and the center is still slightly soft and jiggly.

6 Remove from the oven. Let stand for 1 minute, then carefully invert the ramekins onto plates. Count to 10, then carefully lift the ramekins off the cakes. Serve immediately with ice cream, a dusting of confectioners' sugar, fresh berries, or all three, if desired.

BAKE SQUAD

Spicy Chocolate Cookies

On the "Sweet and Spicy Fiesta" episode of *Bake Squad*, chef Christina Tosi's team of pastry rock stars—Ashley Holt, Christophe Rull, Maya-Camille Broussard, and Gonzo Jimenez—create jaw-dropping desserts they hope will be served at the 60th birthday party of a hot-sauce-loving dad named Pedro.

Inspired by Pedro's love of both sweet and heat and the *Bake Squad*'s showstopping desserts, we've created these loaded triple-chocolate cookies. Deeply chocolatey, our cookies get a gentle kick from chipotle chili powder, cayenne pepper, and ground ginger.

YIELD: 20 cookies
PREP TIME: 25 minutes, plus softening and chilling
COOK TIME: 30 minutes

🌿 VEGETARIAN

5 tablespoons unsalted butter

½ cup unsweetened coconut flakes

½ cup pecans

1 cup all-purpose flour

¼ cup unsweetened Dutch process cocoa powder

1 teaspoon baking powder

¾ teaspoon ground cinnamon

½ teaspoon chipotle chili powder

¼ teaspoon ground ginger

¼ teaspoon cayenne pepper

⅛ teaspoon ground cardamom

½ teaspoon salt

8 ounces bittersweet chocolate, finely chopped

½ teaspoon espresso powder

¾ cup light brown sugar

¼ cup granulated sugar

1½ teaspoons pure vanilla extract

2 large eggs

½ cup white chocolate chips

½ cup semisweet chocolate chips

1 Preheat the oven to 325°F/163°C with racks in the center and upper third positions. Place the butter on the counter for about 40 minutes to soften. On a rimmed baking sheet, spread the coconut flakes in an even layer on one half of the sheet, then place the pecans on the other half. Transfer the baking sheet to the center rack, then bake for 5 to 7 minutes, until lightly browned and fragrant. Remove from the oven and cool. Coarsely chop the pecans.

2 To a medium bowl, add the flour, cocoa powder, baking powder, cinnamon, chili powder, ginger, cayenne, cardamom, and salt, then whisk to combine.

3 Place the bittersweet chocolate in a microwave-safe bowl. Microwave at 50% power in 30-second increments until melted. Sprinkle the espresso powder over the chocolate, then stir until the espresso has dissolved and the chocolate is smooth. Let cool to room temperature.

4 Cut the softened butter into smaller pieces, then add to a large bowl. Using a hand mixer, beat the butter on medium speed for about 1 minute, until light and fluffy. Add the light brown sugar and granulated sugar to the same bowl, then beat on medium speed for about 1 minute, until just incorporated. (The mixture will look grainy and this is okay.) Add the vanilla. Crack the eggs into the same bowl, one at a time, beating on low speed until just combined.

>>recipe continues on the next page

>>Spicy Chocolate Cookies continued

5 Beating the cookie batter on low, add the melted bittersweet chocolate in a steady stream. Use a rubber spatula to stir the mixture until just combined. Sprinkle the dry ingredients over the batter, then stir until just combined. Fold in the toasted coconut, pecans, white and semisweet chocolate chips. Cover the bowl with plastic wrap, then transfer to the refrigerator for about 30 minutes, until slightly firm. Increase the oven heat to 350°F/177°C.

6 Line two rimmed baking sheets with parchment paper. Scoop out 2-tablespoon balls of cookie dough and place them on the baking sheets about 2 inches apart.

7 Transfer to the upper and middle racks of the oven. Bake until the cookies are just set but the centers are still quite soft, 8 to 10 minutes, rotating the baking sheets from back to front and top to bottom halfway through cooking.

8 Remove the cookies from the oven. Cool on the baking sheets for 10 minutes, then carefully transfer the parchment and the cookies to wire cooling racks. Cool for 10 to 15 minutes to room temperature.

9 The cookies can be stored in a sealed container at room temperature for 3 days.

SEX EDUCATION

A Cake for Aimee

During the third season of *Sex Education*, newly inspired baker Aimee makes a pink bunny birthday cake for Maeve. If Maeve were to bake a cake for Aimee, we think it would look a lot like this sweet, whimsical jelly-doughnut cake. In our recipe, this tender buttermilk Bundt cake is filled with warm apricot jam and topped with a swoop of colorful frosting and a happy dusting of sprinkles.

YIELD: 1 Bundt cake   **PREP TIME:** 15 minutes
COOK TIME: 1 hour 10 minutes

🌿 **VEGETARIAN**

Nonstick baking spray for greasing

1 cup unsalted butter

4 large eggs

1 cup buttermilk

3 cups all-purpose flour

2½ teaspoons baking powder

2 teaspoons freshly grated nutmeg

1 teaspoon plus a pinch of kosher salt, divided

½ teaspoon baking soda

1¼ cups granulated sugar

1¾ teaspoons pure vanilla extract, divided

1½ cups apricot jam

1½ cups confectioners' sugar

1 to 2 tablespoons whole milk

Orange or yellow food coloring

Sprinkles for decorating

1. Coat a 12-cup Bundt pan with nonstick baking spray. Place the butter, eggs, and buttermilk on the counter for about 40 minutes to come to room temperature. Preheat the oven to 350°F/177°C with a rack in the center position. In a medium bowl, add the flour, baking powder, nutmeg, 1 teaspoon of the salt, and baking soda, then whisk to combine.

2. In a large bowl or the bowl of a stand mixer fitted with a paddle attachment, combine the butter and sugar, then beat on medium speed for 3 to 4 minutes, until light and fluffy. Add the eggs one at a time, beating well after each addition. Beat in 1½ teaspoons of the vanilla. On low speed, alternate adding the dry ingredients and the buttermilk, starting and ending with the dry ingredients. Mix until just combined.

3. Scrape the batter into the prepared Bundt pan, then smooth the top with a spatula. Transfer to the oven, then bake for about 1 hour, until the cake springs back lightly to the touch and a toothpick or skewer inserted into the cake comes out clean. Place the cake on a wire rack and cool for 15 minutes.

4. Meanwhile, add the jam to a microwave-safe liquid measuring cup. Microwave on high in 15-second increments until the jam is warm and pourable.

5. After the cake has cooled, use a wooden spoon to poke 2-inch deep holes about ½ inch apart around the center of the cake. Wipe off the spoon handle after making each hole. Divide the jam among the holes, then let the cake cool completely, for about 1 hour.

6. Carefully invert the Bundt cake onto a plate or cake stand. Sift the confectioners' sugar into a bowl, then add 1 tablespoon of the milk, the remaining ¼ teaspoon of vanilla, and a pinch of salt. Whisk the glaze until smooth, adding another tablespoon of milk if the glaze feels too thick. Add the food coloring, a drop at a time, until the desired color is achieved. Spoon the glaze over the cake, then decorate with the sprinkles.

Nailed It!

You Nailed It Cake

How hard is it really for a home cook to re-create the awe-inspiring, often gravity-defying, crave-worthy sweets that we see online and on our favorite shows? As it turns out, pretty hard. On the show *Nailed It!* hosts Chef Jacques Torres and comedian Nicole Byer coach, laugh, and cheer on three hopefuls each week who are trying to re-create next-level bakes in real time.

As we learned from *Nailed It!*, the desserts don't just need to look good, they need to taste good, too. And since time is a factor in competitions, you want to get the cakes and frosting finished quickly enough so that you can get started on your decorations. Our *Nailed It!* creations start with a quick, no-mixer-required vanilla cake and a classic fluffy vanilla buttercream.

As for the decorations, you have buttercream and your dreams! While we made a Netflix cake to celebrate our cookbook, you can make fondant animals, get creative with food coloring, make daring caramel creations inspired by your favorite shows. We've included a bonus recipe on page 177 for a crisped rice cereal treat, perfect for slicing or shaping.

YIELD: One 9-inch, 3-layer cake
PREP TIME: 45 minutes, plus softening
COOK TIME: 30 minutes, plus cooling

 VEGETARIAN

CAKE LAYERS

1 cup plus 2 tablespoons unsalted butter

6 large eggs

1½ cups whole milk

Nonstick baking spray for greasing

4½ cups cake flour

⅔ cup granulated sugar

2¼ teaspoons baking powder

1 teaspoon kosher salt

½ teaspoon pure vanilla extract

VANILLA BUTTERCREAM

1½ cups unsalted butter

4 cups confectioners' sugar

¼ teaspoon kosher salt

4 to 5 tablespoons heavy cream

2 teaspoons pure vanilla extract

>>recipe continues on the next page

Want to customize the cake inside *and* out?
To the cake batter, you can stir in ⅔ cup toasted and finely chopped nuts; 3 tablespoons fresh citrus zest; or 1 tablespoon ground cinnamon, 1 teaspoon ground ginger, and ⅛ teaspoon ground nutmeg. You can spread ⅓ cup of lemon curd, jam, chocolate hazelnut spread, or salted caramel between the layers.

>>You Nailed It Cake continued

1 **To make the cakes:** In a medium saucepan, heat the butter over medium for about 5 minutes, until melted. Remove from the heat and cool completely. Place the eggs and milk on the counter for about 40 minutes to come to room temperature.

2 Preheat the oven to 350°F/177°C with a rack in the center position. Coat three 9-inch cake pans with nonstick baking spray, then line the bottom of each pan with a circle of parchment paper. In a large bowl, add the flour, sugar, baking powder, and salt, then whisk to combine.

3 In a medium bowl, add the eggs, then whisk until the yolks and whites are combined. Add the melted butter, milk, and vanilla extract to the same bowl, then whisk to combine. Add the wet ingredients to the dry, then mix with a rubber spatula until just combined. (A few lumps are okay.)

4 Divide the cake batter among the cake pans, then smooth the tops with a spatula. Transfer the cakes to the oven, then bake for 25 to 30 minutes, until the cakes spring back lightly to the touch.

5 Remove the cakes from the oven. Cool for 10 minutes, then invert onto wire racks and peel off the parchment. Flip the cakes back over so the top side is up. Cool completely before decorating.

6 **To make the vanilla buttercream:** Place the butter on the counter for about 40 minutes to come to room temperature. Sift the confectioners' sugar to remove any lumps.

7 Cut the softened butter into ½-inch pieces. In a large bowl or the bowl of a stand mixer fitted with a paddle attachment, combine the butter, confectioners' sugar, and salt. Beat on medium speed for about 5 minutes, until light and fluffy. To the same bowl, add 3 tablespoons of the heavy cream and the vanilla, then continue beating for 1 to 2 minutes, until combined and fluffy. Add more cream, 1 tablespoon at a time, if the buttercream is too thick.

8 Using a serrated knife, trim off the domed tops of the cake layers. Transfer one cake layer, cut side up, to a cake stand or platter. Place ⅔ cup of the buttercream on top of the cake, then spread into an even layer. Repeat with the second and third cake layers, spreading ⅔ cup buttercream between each layer. Coat the top and sides of the cake with a thin layer of buttercream, then transfer to the refrigerator for about 30 minutes, until the frosting is firm.

9 Decorate the cake with the remaining buttercream as you see fit, making judges Chef Jacques Torres and comedian Nicole Byer proud. Then reveal the finished cake with a flourish, yelling "Nailed It!"

Crisped Rice Cereal Layer

On the "Fantasyland" episode of *Nailed It!,* the contestants made princess towers using cake layers and a crisped rice cereal mixture for both boulders and the tower. We were inspired by the amazing decorating feats, so we added a bonus recipe for you. If you want to add a big red Netflix logo, a rounded dome, a unicorn horn, or another sculptural element to your *Nailed It!* cake, the rice cereal shapes covered with buttercream or fondant will help your cake achieve new heights.

BONUS RECIPE!

CRISPED RICE CEREAL LAYER FOR MOLDING/ SHAPING

¼ cup white chocolate melts

8 ounces marshmallows (about 30 marshmallows)

4 to 6 cups crisped rice cereal (chocolate rice cereal works here too)

¾ teaspoon kosher salt

Nonstick baking spray or vegetable shortening for greasing

Fondant, modeling chocolate, or buttercream for decorating

1 Add the white chocolate melts to a medium microwave-safe bowl. Microwave on 50% power in 15-second increments until mostly melted, then stir until smooth. Set aside for step 2.

2 Add the marshmallows to a large microwave-safe bowl. Microwave on high, in 10-second increments, until the marshmallows are almost all melted. Remove the bowl from the microwave, then stir until smooth. Immediately add 4 cups of the crisped rice cereal, then stir until evenly coated in the marshmallows. Scrape the melted white chocolate into the same bowl, then add the salt. Stir until combined.

3 The cereal should be evenly coated in the marshmallow–white chocolate mixture, but it should not be too wet or gloopy. If necessary, add more crisped rice cereal, ½ cup at a time, until the desired consistency is achieved.

4 **To sculpt into shapes:** Let the cereal mixture stand at room temperature for 5 minutes. Spray your hands with nonstick spray or rub with vegetable shortening, then use your hands to pack the cereal mixture into the desired shapes. (Squeeze the mixture as you go. A more tightly packed shape will be less likely to crumble.) Chill until firm, about 15 minutes, then decorate with fondant, modeling chocolate, or buttercream.

5 **To cut into shapes:** Lightly coat a 9-by-13-inch baking pan with nonstick spray, then line the bottom and sides with plastic wrap, leaving 2 inches of plastic wrap hanging over each of two sides. Coat again with nonstick spray. Scrape the cereal into the prepared pan, then press into a firm, even layer with lightly greased hands. Transfer to the refrigerator, then chill for about 45 minutes, until very firm.

6 Using the plastic wrap overhang, lift the cereal sheet out of the baking dish, then invert onto a cutting board. Peel off the plastic wrap, then cut into shapes. Decorate with fondant, modeling chocolate, or buttercream.

Index of Shows

INSIGHT
EDITIONS

PO Box 3088
San Rafael, CA 94912
www.insighteditions.com

 Find us on Facebook:
www.facebook.com/InsightEditions
 Follow us on Twitter: @insighteditions
 Follow us on Instagram: @insighteditions

NETFLIX

ISBN: 978-1-64722-949-8

INSIGHT EDITIONS
Publisher: Raoul Goff
VP, Co-Publisher: Vanessa Lopez
VP, Creative: Chrissy Kwasnik
VP, Manufacturing: Alix Nicholaeff
VP, Group Managing Editor: Vicki Jaeger
Publishing Director: Jamie Thompson
Senior Editor: Samantha Holland
Editorial Assistant: Sami Alvarado
Design Support: Megan Sinead Bingham
Managing Editor: Maria Spano
Senior Production Editor: Katie Rokakis
Production Associate: Deena Hashem
Senior Production Manager,
Subsidiary Rights: Lina s Palma-Temena

INDELIBLE
EDITIONS

Produced by INDELIBLE EDITIONS
Editorial Director: Dinah Dunn
Photographer: Beryl Striewski
Recipe Tester: Rob Stella

Illustrations by: Adam Raiti

ROOTS of PEACE   REPLANTED PAPER

Insight Editions, in association with Roots of Peace, will plant two trees for each tree used in the manufacturing of this book. Roots of Peace is an internationally renowned humanitarian organization dedicated to eradicating land mines worldwide and converting war-torn lands into productive farms and wildlife habitats. Roots of Peace will plant two million fruit and nut trees in Afghanistan and provide farmers there with the skills and support necessary for sustainable land use.

Manufactured in China by Insight Editions

10 9 8 7 6 5 4 3 2 1

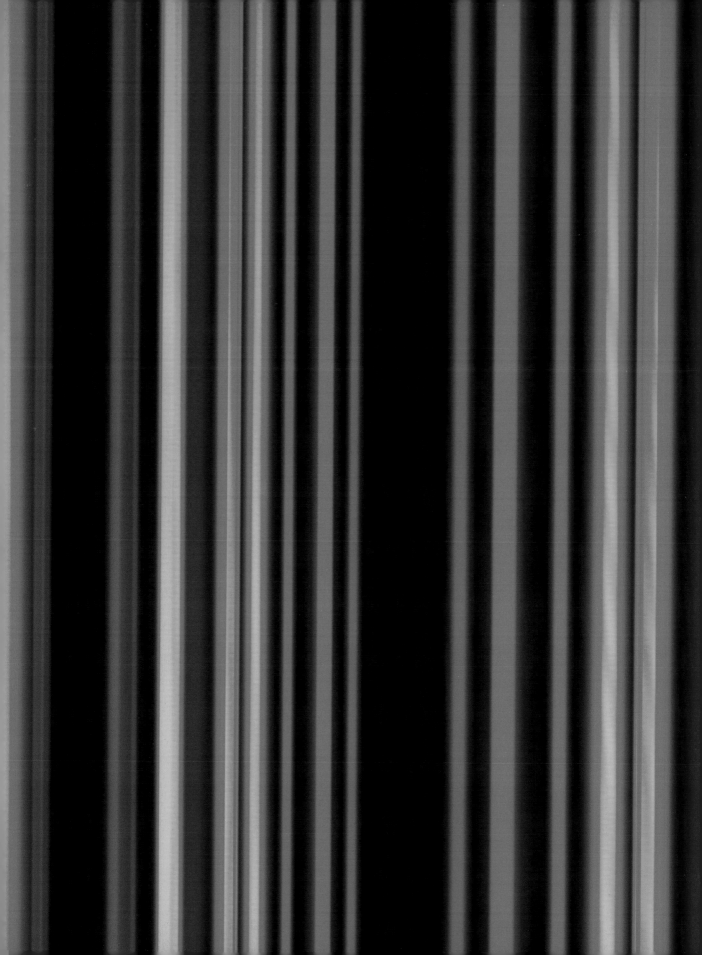

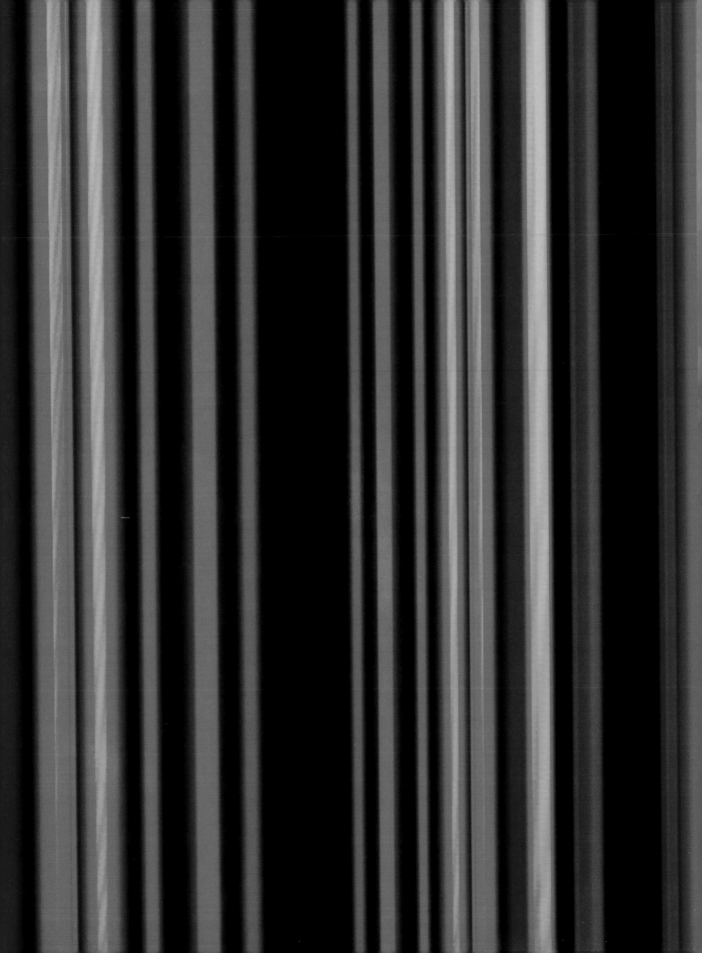